THE PACIFIC SALMON FISHERIES

A Study of Irrational Conservation

The
PACIFIC
SALMON
FISHERIES

A Study of Irrational Conservation

JAMES A. CRUTCHFIELD
and GIULIO PONTECORVO

Published for RESOURCES FOR THE FUTURE, INC.
by THE JOHNS HOPKINS PRESS

James A. Crutchfield is professor of economics at the University of
Washington. Giulio Pontecorvo is professor of economics and banking
at the Graduate School of Business, Columbia University. The manuscript was edited by Marta Erdman. Charts were drawn by Clare and
Frank Ford. The index was prepared by Adele Garrett.

RFF editors: Henry Jarrett, Vera W. Dodds, Nora E. Roots,
Sheila M. Ekers.

Foreword

~~~~~~

Fisheries in the United States are beset by senseless restrictions and marked by obsolescence, waste, and poverty. The contribution of fishermen to the national economy is negligible. Their total catch of all species is lower now than it was before the Second World War. And there is little hope for change—unless dramatically new institutions and new forms of management can be developed and adopted.

The fundamental cause of waste is open access to the stocks. Where resources are unowned or the common property of a community, there are no controls over access; no means for allocating or restricting inputs of capital and labor; and no way of preventing declining yields and the disappearance of net revenues to the industry. These consequences are particularly severe for fisheries, where demand is increasing and natural factors limit the rate of reproduction and the size of the stock. And the problems are frequently compounded by the adoption of conservation measures that impede technological innovation and make fishing more difficult and more costly.

The theory of common property resources has been explored

by a handful of economists over the past fifteen years. But little has been done to apply the theory to real fisheries or to develop and test models that co-ordinate biologic and economic functions and conditions. Indeed, aside from studies of Pacific halibut (by Crutchfield and Arnold Zellner), Georges Bank haddock, and one or two smaller fisheries, there have been virtually no empirical analyses of the economic consequences of common property in fisheries. Partly as a result of the paucity of case studies and factual demonstrations of waste, the fishery administrators have been reluctant to accept the theory and adopt the new institutions and new forms of management that are required.

This book thus provides an important contribution to the field. It demonstrates the consequences of open access and irrational conservation; develops a model that can be used in other case studies; and sets the framework for control of access and for the establishment of effective conservation rules and efficient economic measures.

This project is a significant element in the emerging marine resources program at Resources for the Future. It follows an earlier and more general study, *The Common Wealth in Ocean Fisheries,* by Francis T. Christy, Jr. and Anthony Scott, and deals directly with some of the problems identified in that study. It also bears a general relationship to a current project being undertaken within the program—a study of the law of the continental shelf by Professor L. F. E. Goldie. The relationship lies in the problems created by the fact that ownership of marine resources is frequently either non-specific or non-existent, and that because of this there are no clear-cut authorities or agencies to govern use and exploitation. This is true for the multiple uses of estuaries, the resources of the sea floor, and for international fisheries as well as domestic.

The demands on the sea are growing rapidly. Oil exploitation, taking place in deeper and deeper waters, is forcing nations to reach decisions on the extent of their jurisdiction and on the character of an international regime beyond their limits. Those nations that have rationalized their fisheries and achieved access controls (particularly Japan and the U.S.S.R.) have gained great mobility and are able to fish in all corners of the world. And as their effectiveness increases, the problems of open access in international waters become increasingly severe. Conflicts between different uses of the sea are also growing. Shipping must thread its way through oil rigs and through concentrations of trawlers. The pressures on estuaries from pollution, land-fill, dredging, recreation, fishing, and other developments, are becoming increasingly apparent and are indicative of problems that must be resolved in both domestic and international waters.

The real challenge of the seas lies in these kinds of problems. Science and technology can open up opportunities that we have scarcely begun to anticipate. But at the same time they create great difficulties for management and for co-operation among the users; for law and efficient rules and regulations; and for the orderly and harmonious enjoyment of the resources of Davy Jones's locker.

These challenges provide the focus for our program. We hope to increase our knowledge about the developments in the marine environment, so that we can anticipate the economic and political pressures that will take place in the future. We want to examine alternative objectives, so that we can know more precisely what it is that we want to gain from the oceans. And we want to begin to explore the institutions and rules that will accommodate the growing pressures and facilitate the attainment of the goals.

These are tasks for economists, lawyers, and scholars of political science and international relations. They are difficult tasks, but extremely important. And it is hoped that this book, in addition to making its contribution to the study of fisheries economics, will stimulate social scientists to explore the problems of the marine environment and to participate in their resolution.

Francis T. Christy, Jr.
Marine Resources Project
Resources for the Future, Inc.

December 1968

Contents

FIGURES

THE PACIFIC SALMON FISHERIES

A Study of Irrational Conservation

CHAPTER 1

The Issues

~~~~~~

While it is true that a great deal (perhaps the greater part) of what has been done in the name of "conservation policy" turns out, upon subjection to economic analysis, to be worthless, or worse, it is nevertheless also true that economic theory can offer a formulation of the conservation objective sufficiently clear and precise to permit the derivation of rational policies in the future. Such a formulation, like the application of economic theory in other fields of policy, can be no match for the passionate romanticism with which the question has been invested in political platforms and public discussion, but some of the policies of the past and present are sufficiently egregious to convince even dedicated conservationists of their error or, at least, insufficiency. Perhaps it is too much to hope that in their hour of confusion and despair, the protectors of nature might turn to economics for succor, but even idealistic hopes have the quality of springing eternal.[1]

In the broadest meaning of the term, wise use of natural resources implies evaluation of their present worth in a dynamic setting of general equilibrium. In this sense, of course, proper use of natural resources can hardly be separated from the allocation problem as a whole. Given assumptions as to rates of eco-

[1] H. Scott Gordon, "Economics and the Conservation Question," *Journal of Law and Economics*, I (October 1958), pp. 110–11.

nomic growth, patterns of demand and costs, and relative prices of substitute and complementary products, conservation of any natural resource clearly is an aspect of capital theory, involving optimal time rates of use of the assets involved and optimal factor combinations at each use rate. The essential problem from the policy standpoint is to avoid waste through faulty time distribution of use of natural resources or through inefficient combinations of their services with those of labor and capital, and hence to maximize the present value of the stream of net benefits that can be derived from them. Beyond this lies the task of applying these general principles to specific resources, specific management programs, and specific proposals for more effective utilization of the physical environment. This study of the Pacific salmon fisheries is an effort in that direction.

In the simplest case, where stocks of the resource are known and fixed in total quantity, optimal time-rate of use is the only issue, since a flow of useful services can be obtained only by using up the stock. At the opposite extreme, resources that provide a flow of services unaffected by varying rates of use present no conservation problem. These are, of course, limiting cases only, hardly to be found in the real world. Policy problems with respect to conservation are usually derived from two intermediate cases. In the first, the stock of resources is finite, but the total magnitude is unknown. In this case, the conservation problem is twofold: first, to assure the most efficient use of known stocks; and second, to undertake that amount of investment in discovery and preparation for extraction which, together with the time rate of use of existing supplies, maximizes the present value of the resource.

The second general case involves resources that are renewable, but only over an extended period of time. In these cases, the twofold nature of the conservation problem is even more clear-cut. The stock, viewed as an inventory to be used as economically as possible, is also the capital equipment, investment in which will provide for replenishment in the future. Clearly, optimal time rates of use involve both efficient conversion of part of the existing stock to current economic output, and the appropriate reservation of part of the stock for production of future supplies.

4

The distinction between stock and renewable resources in these terms is perhaps less clear-cut than the brief summary above suggests. It involves, among others, some implicit assumptions about future costs and prices. If we assume that the end product of a given natural resource—a fishery population, for example—will become obsolescent before the yield from new "investment" (in the sense of restricted current use) is realized, the resource becomes in effect a pure stock resource, and the conservation problem becomes one of using up the existing stock over the appropriate period of time. Similarly, if costs are expected to rise to a level at which there will be no profit from the resource no matter what the output, there is clearly no point in "conserving" in the investment sense.

These are, however, exceptions to an obviously common and important group of resource utilization problems involving renewable stocks for which maximization of present value requires simultaneous evaluation of current and potential future exploitation rates on a continuous basis. Most fishery populations fall in this category, and this study is concerned with one of the major fisheries in which conservation programming has proved essential to avoid complete destruction of the resource—biological as well as economic.

Scope of the Study

There are many reasons for choosing the Pacific salmon industry to illustrate the essential principles of an integrated fishery management program aimed at economic maximization of benefits from the resource and also to demonstrate a contrast between optimal and actual results of management. First, it is one of the most valuable of North American fisheries, and ranks high in value among individual fisheries of the world. The stakes, in terms of regional welfare, are sufficiently high to make this study more than an academic exercise, particularly in Alaska. Second, the physical functions relating investment in salmon stocks to subsequent flows of fish available for capture and the associated functions relating fishing effort to short- and long-run yield are probably more complex in the case of the Pacific salmon than in any other major exploited fishery. Despite

5

this complexity, management of the Pacific salmon has evolved far enough—both in its economic and in its political dimensions—to provide a usable statistical record of the physical magnitudes involved, and sufficient economic information has been generated to permit evaluation of the overall programs.

Space and time limitations preclude detailed analysis of the characteristics of the entire North American salmon fishery and the complex regulatory programs of the Pacific Coast states and of Canada (which regulates the British Columbia fishery); to do so would also involve much needless repetition. We have, therefore, focused our attention on the salmon fisheries of Alaska and Puget Sound. The Alaska fisheries present a classic case of overfishing, unalloyed with any of the other factors—pollution, deforestation, and other man-made changes in environment—which usually cloud causal analysis of declining yields. The Puget Sound sockeye and pink runs, centered on the famous Fraser River populations, illustrate the economic impact of an intensive research program and a nearly unique case of international cooperation set against a background of a full cycle of substantial depletion and subsequent partial rehabilitation. Together, the Alaska and Puget Sound fisheries account for about 90 percent of the U.S. catch of salmon and 60 to 70 percent of the total North American salmon catch by value. Between them, they illustrate virtually all of the technological and biological complexities that beset both the salmon fishing industry and the management authorities.

The stakes in salmon conservation are worthy of careful thought. Even at the depleted levels of the 1960's, the annual gross value of the Pacific salmon catch to American and Canadian fishermen has averaged over $60 million. The vicious and continuous political infighting that has plagued the conservation authorities from Alaska to the Columbia River is eloquent testimony to the participants' awareness of economic considerations in fishery management. Yet there is little evidence that the development of scientific research-oriented regulation was accompanied by any substantive awareness of the crucial importance of economic factors.

Our central theme is that rational fishery management must

evolve from the objective of maximizing the net *economic* yield of the resource. One reason for this approach is that the traditional definition of regulatory objectives in purely physical terms has left conservation authorities vulnerable to political pressures by denying them a vital basis for choice. The vulnerability comes about in the following way: a fishery shows biological evidence of "overfishing," i.e., aggregate yields may fall, the amplitude of annual oscillations in yield may increase, or—more probably— both phenomena are observed. At the same time, generally in response to an improvement in earnings as a result of a positive income elasticity of demand, fishing effort is increased. In order to protect the resource, the administrative body created to deal with the problem of "overfishing" must reduce fishing mortality. Since the fishery is an open access resource, it is impossible under current conditions to reduce effort by restricting the inputs. The regulators cannot stop more people using more equipment from going fishing. In this situation, the obvious alternative is to reduce progressively the efficiency of the individual inputs and thereby reduce the pressure exerted on the resource by a growing number of fishing units. The resulting drift into greater and greater inefficiency in the use of human and capital resources erodes both control and compliance; and the concomitant deterioration of capital equipment leaves the industry increasingly vulnerable to competition, both foreign and domestic. At the same time, the basic irrationality of legislated inefficiency tends to cause widespread discouragement and cynicism in the industry. Failure to develop regulations based on an economic calculus leads to the *ad hoc*, "hole-plugging" hodgepodge of regulations now characteristic of many fisheries. It is important to realize that the need for regulation of open access fisheries arises from economic reactions of profit-seeking units. If this fact is realized, a simple, consistent, and readily enforceable program can be developed.

The setting for any management of salmon resources is both physical and institutional. On one side is a set of complex biological problems: How is it possible to manage the population dynamics of an organism that lives in an environment over which the biologist has little control in order to approximate a chosen

7

level of physical yield from the resource? On the other side, the question arises: How can this be accomplished within the constraints of a given set of legal and social institutions, which lead, in the absence of intervention, to gross inefficiency and waste in the use of both human and physical capital? Clearly, any meaningful solution for the problems of a commercial fishery must account for both these facets of its structure. From the standpoint of time and money, the research required to define and quantify the essential physical relations that determine available yield is far more demanding than the economic analysis. Yet both are essential to any conservation program that could be considered a rational effort to increase the contribution of the resource to human welfare. Productive fish stocks are a necessary, but not a sufficient, condition for optimal use of those stocks.

ORGANIZATION OF THE STUDY

In the following chapters we hope to demonstrate the essential validity of this statement. To do so, we develop first a general model of a commercial fishery. Production functions—and, therefore, economic supply functions—are derived from a biological model of a fish population. Given these functions, it is possible to specify the necessary and sufficient conditions for the maximization of the net economic yield from the resource. The model, in this form, is then utilized to discuss the theoretical basis of a wide range of performance characteristics associated with commercial fisheries.

The most important of these calls for an explanation of the persistent failure of a competitive structure to maximize welfare under conditions of free entry to an open access resource. From this basic premise, Chapter 2 examines the problems of valuation of an industry in which long-run equilibrium is reached only at zero net economic yield. In addition, we consider the implications of heavy overcapitalization for the cyclical performance of the industry.

Following the exposition of the relevant theoretical issues, we present two case studies of Pacific salmon fisheries. The primary objective of these studies is to test the hypotheses advanced in Chapter 2. This process requires elaboration of the historical development of these fisheries in terms quite different from those that have been advanced elsewhere.

Chapter 3 provides a summary of all major types of gear employed in catching Pacific salmon and a description of each of the regulatory measures that have been used to control fishing mortality. The next three chapters are devoted to the development and structure of the Alaska salmon fishery and to the management programs that have been devised to deal with its problems. In Chapter 7, a technique is developed and applied to measure the potential economic rent from one of the most important segments of the Alaska fishery, the Bristol Bay red (sockeye) salmon operation.

Chapters 8 and 9 carry forward the same analysis with respect to the Puget Sound salmon fishery. The history and structure of the fishery and of the regulatory program are analyzed in Chapter 8, while Chapter 9 presents a calculation of potential net economic yield using a different technique than that employed in the Bristol Bay case.

Chapter 10 brings together the threads of the earlier discussion, and extends the estimates of net economic rent to other salmon-producing areas in North America. On the basis of the conclusion that the economic waste implicit in present methods of regulation is large enough to warrant serious concern, the elements of a salmon-management program, geared to maximum net economic yield as the prime objective, are then developed. The impact of Japanese high-seas fisheries for salmon on any management program that may be devised is also considered. In Chapter 11, our conclusions are compared to those reached in other case studies of marine fisheries, and the implications of these findings for subsequent world development of marine resources are noted.

Only passing attention has been given the sport fishery, despite its increasing economic significance, because the introduction of another type of human predation upon the salmon does not alter the fundamental conclusions reached. Where appropriate, however, reference has been made to the overlapping of sport and commercial activities, and to the implications for optimal regulatory programs.

For the same reason, relatively little attention has been paid the troll fishery. Although commercial trollers take a large and increasing proportion of the total catch of chinook and silver salmon (the great bulk of it for sale in the fresh and frozen market), they are, for all practical purposes, virtually free of regulation at the present. Moreover, the total troll catch is still very small in relation to the total North American salmon catch.

We feel that an analysis in economic terms of the history and practice of management in the salmon fisheries is a project well worth doing in its own right. There is much to be learned from a more precise explanation of the interaction of economic structure, resource characteristics, and regulatory technique. It is also highly significant, however, that the results of our study conform closely to those of a number of other investigations of fisheries and management programs of entirely different types. As indicated in the concluding chapter, the disappointing results of the conservation effort in the Pacific salmon fishery stem from structural defects in institutional arrangements and regulatory concepts, which are of far greater potential significance when viewed in a worldwide context. The pace of technological change in the high-seas fisheries is rapidly sweeping aside national and regional boundaries. Poor economic performance of the fisheries is not simply a result of the complex biological characteristics of particular fish stocks or peculiarities of the geographic area in which the fishery is prosecuted. What has happened in the salmon fishery now threatens all fisheries where the prices of end products relative to harvesting costs provide sufficient incentive to convert fish stocks to economic goods. The prospective growth in the demand for animal proteins, coupled with the tremendous impact of new capital investment in modern fishing vessels and gear in European and Asian countries, promises to provide just such incentives.

CHAPTER 2

Bio-Economic Models of Exploited Fisheries

~~~~~~

Throughout the world, both within national economies and on the high seas, there are important resources that are not owned by anyone. In almost all cases the exploitation of these unowned resources is on a basis of competitive withdrawal: a basis which differentiates the usage of common property (or, more properly, open access) resources from that of private property in general.[1] Both classical and neoclassical economists have noted, and in some cases discussed at length, this distinction. In the debate over "empty economic boxes" in the early 1920's, Frank H. Knight clearly specified the issues involved.[2]

---

[1] The term "common property," as it has been used by economists, is incorrect in a strict legal sense. If a resource is not owned, it is not property. We will, therefore, employ the term "open access resources."

Professor Donald F. Gordon has informed us that in the annals of the Mecklenburg Agricultural Society in the 1820's, J. H. von Thünen gave an extended analysis of the open access resource problem. The basic article in the current economic literature is the original contribution of H. Scott Gordon, "The Economic Theory of a Common Property Resource: The Fishery," *Journal of Political Economy*, 62 (April 1954), pp. 124–42.

[2] Frank H. Knight, "Some Fallacies in the Interpretation of Social Cost," *Quarterly Journal of Economics*, XXXVIII (1924), pp. 582–606. Reprinted in *Readings in Price Theory*, G. J. Stigler and K. E. Boulding (eds.) (Richard D. Irwin, Inc., 1952), pp. 160–79.

The statement does in fact indicate what would happen if no one owned the superior farm. But under private appropriation and self-seeking exploitation of the land the course of events is very different. It is in fact the social function of ownership to prevent this excessive investment in superior situations.[3]

The economic literature has usually lumped all problems of misallocation of resources, in a competitive situation, under the externalities argument.[4] External diseconomies are certainly present in most, if not all, fisheries. For example, true lobsters, at younger adult ages, moult (shed their shell) roughly once a year. Since each moult represents about a 15 percent growth, every year there is a new class (stock) of entrants into the fishery as a moult group grows to legal size. Predation by fishermen on this stock clearly involves external diseconomies for each firm (fisherman) as one man's catch raises the cost of capture for the rest.

To stop the analysis at this point, however, is to miss the essential problem involved in the exploitation of an open access resource. The key to the distinction between the open access resource and, for example, agriculture lies in the institutional arrangements relating to ownership of the resource. In the fisheries, Knight's "social function of ownership" is not performed.

As we shall explain, in the case of open access resources— under certain assumptions applicable to most of the world's fisheries—the misallocation of resources results from overexploitation. In these cases, exploitation is pushed to the point where average unit costs are equal to price exclusive of rent. In these circumstances, the economic rent inherent in "superior situations" is dissipated to pay the opportunity incomes of the additional entrants.

In addition, the productive capacity of a fish stock is limited. It may therefore be expected that this situation will grow steadily

[3] *Ibid.,* p. 163.
[4] W. S. Baumol, *Economic Theory and Operations Analysis* (2d ed.; Prentice-Hall, Inc., 1965), p. 369. In our view, this simplification stems in part from the difficulty of applying the usual diagrammatics of the firm to the open access case.

worse as prices of heavily exploited fisheries rise and pressure shifts to other species and other localities.

In its ultimate form, a systematic economic theory of open access resources must distinguish open access problems as an addition to the usual classification of market structures, examine systematically the role of rent in the exploitation of these resources, and integrate economic production theory with the diverse physical constraints on exploitation that are inherent in the nature of specific open access resources. So far, however, it has not gone much beyond the beginnings. This hiatus is explained in part by the possibility, at least in the past, of devising workable approximations to conditions of private ownership, or of actual alienation from open access to private ownership. Historically, the difficult transition in Europe from the open fields and community property of the medieval manor to the contemporary system of land utilization provides an interesting and well-documented case. In the United States attention has centered on the problem of subsurface oil pools and subsequent efforts at a partial solution embodied in the proration programs of the states. The earlier ravaging of forest and grazing lands, under essentially open access status, has given way to conscious management, at least partially oriented to maximization of net economic yield, by the U.S. Forest Service and Bureau of Land Management (as managers of public lands) and by private timber operators.

In recent years, a series of resource utilization problems, for which partial solutions of these types are not technically feasible, have come to the fore. The most intriguing—and, at the moment, the most significant—involve the resources of the oceans. In a narrower sphere, some of the most vexing valuation problems in the area of benefit-cost analysis—particularly those involving recreational uses of land and water—are bound up in the economics of open access resources.

The critical issues involved in both theoretical and applied analysis of optimal usage of open access resources are all illustrated in the case to be discussed in this study: the salmon fisheries of the Pacific Coast. Moreover, these fisheries are of more than casual importance in the world scene, as evidenced by the speed with which the race to engage in salmon fishing on the high seas has developed and the bitterness of the resulting international conflicts (disputes between the United States and Canada date from 1900), not to mention some equally clamorous disputes among the Pacific Coast states.

The theoretical work on the fisheries by professional economists falls into two phases. In the early period, roughly the 1950's, the chief concern was over the initial articulation of the problem and the formulation of models that emphasized the dissipation of economic rent. Unfortunately, at the same time, this discussion left in limbo a number of related questions that must be dealt with in a more general analytical framework. One concerns the nature of the relevant production functions. In his pioneering article, Gordon assumed a very simple yield-effort model that is far from general. A second deficiency was the failure to explore fully the effects of the unusual characteristics of the production (biological yield) functions associated with fisheries on market structure and performance. It will be argued that some of the key aspects of organization and firm policy in the salmon fisheries may be attributed to the wide and unpredictable fluctuations in yields and the persistent overcapacity that characterizes the fisheries. The effects on the resulting market structures for raw fish extend beyond fishing proper and influence the economic organization and performance of the processing-marketing sector as well.

More recently, in the 1960's, several attempts have been made to reformulate the older models in order to integrate the efforts of the marine biologist and the economist.[5] In this chapter we shall first develop a model of this latter type as a basis for discussion of the range of theoretical issues involved in the combination of economic and biological analysis. Subsequently, the implications of specific biological yield functions applicable to the Pacific salmon fishery will be developed.

[5] See James A. Crutchfield and Arnold Zellner, *Economic Aspects of the Pacific Halibut Fishery*, Fishery Industrial Research, Vol. I (U.S. Department of the Interior, Washington, 1961), chapters 2 and 3, and Appendix I; and R. Turvey, "Optimization in Fishery Regulation," *American Economic Review*, LIV (March 1964), for summaries and bibliographies.

BIOLOGICAL YIELD FUNCTIONS: THE PHYSICAL BASIS OF A FISHERY

Biologists have been engaged in theoretical and empirical study of the characteristics of fish populations since the 1880's. In recent decades, increasingly sophisticated models have been developed to explore the dynamics of exploited fish populations. Most of these have been centered on the determination of long-run equilibrium values, but there has been increasing interest in the time path of the short-term adjustment mechanisms as well. These biological yield functions are of special interest to the economist since they are readily translated into economic production functions.

The first part of the following discussion is couched in terms of a relatively simple "sigmoid curve" yield-effort function of a type underlying much of the previous economic analysis of fisheries.[6] It represents a useful first approximation for descriptive and analytical purposes since the long-run economic characteristics of the model are largely independent of the diverse physical parameters of different ecological systems in which different types of fish exist. This model is, however, essentially static in nature, resting on the assumption that the size of the exploited population and the flow of useful output from it tend toward stable equilibrium values for each level of fishing effort. An operational model of the salmon fishery must encompass a far more difficult biological pattern in which population size may cycle, even with steady rates of fishing, and in which short-term disequilibrium, in both biological and economic terms, is continuous. These considerations, and their economic implications, are developed in the remainder of the chapter.

The commercial fisheries exist as a result of the capacity of the populations exploited to sustain additional predation by man. Unfortunately, the ecological systems of which these stocks

---

[6] There are differences of opinion among biologists as to the utility of alternative formulations, but these differences do not affect the argument presented here. For a summary of the biological literature, evaluation of the various models, and an extensive bibliography, see L. Dickie, "Effects of Regulation of Fish Catches," in *The Economics of Fishery Regulation*, Food and Agriculture Organization of the United Nations, Fisheries Report No. 5, Rome, 1962. The formulation used in this section follows that by M. B. Schaefer.

15

are a part are extremely complex and relatively unstable. The delineation and quantification of yield-effort relations are complicated by a number of characteristics unique to the fisheries. Not the least of these is the problem of measurement. In counting and weighing fish in their free state, biologists are confined to sampling, the cost of which is usually high relative to the value of the outputs involved, or to data recorded by commercial fishermen, which are neither random nor completely free of reporting biases. This does not preclude analysis and quantification of the forces determining the size, composition, and time path of change of a fish population, but it does require caution in generalizing from individual studies.

The problems are multiplied enormously in the case of salmon by the complexity of the life cycle of each species and the high cost of sampling imposed by their wide distribution on the high seas during much of their lives. Present knowledge of their distribution is fairly complete, but the cost of locating salmon on the high seas, sampling to determine sea survival, identifying the areas of origin, and interpreting the data obtained is so high that the combined capabilities of the state, federal, and international agencies now engaged in salmon research cannot forecast as accurately as they could if money were no object. Moreover, since all Pacific salmon die after spawning once, full information on the availability of each year class becomes available only in the very short period in which the fish run the gantlet of the fishery and ascend their spawning streams.

The "steady-state yields" (or, in economic terms, the equilibrium production possibilities) of a fish stock are determined by factors that can be conveniently grouped under four headings: growth rates of individual fish; recruitment of new individuals to the "fishable" stock; mortality originating in the natural environment; and fishing mortality.

Long-term equilibrium in the total size and age composition of a fish stock is reached when marginal increments from growth and recruitment of new individual fish to the exploited phase are exactly offset by the decrements caused by natural mortality and man's own predation.

In Schaefer's terminology, "the outstanding characteristic of populations of fishes and other natural populations of organisms is that they tend to remain in dynamic balance. When, however, the percentage rate of loss is increased, decreasing the size of the population from whatever cause, the percentage rate of renewal must increase also so that the population again comes into balance."[7]

There is, therefore, a schedule of fishing yields consistent with each level of population from zero to the maximum the environment will support. For any given population, equilibrium is reached when the catch equals the rate of natural increase in total biomass. From these relationships Schaefer derives the following yield function:

$$L = k_2 E \left(M - \frac{k_2}{k_1} E \right)$$

where L is landings, E—fishing effort, M—maximum population, and k_1 and k_2 are constants.

The complete model is as follows:[8]

$$\frac{dP}{dt} = f(P) \tag{1}$$

$$L = \phi(P, E) \tag{2}$$

$$P = \psi(E) \tag{3}$$

$$f(P) = k_1 P(M - P) \tag{4}$$

$$L = k_2 EP \tag{5}$$

$$k_2 E P = k_1 P(M - P) \tag{6}$$

$$P = M - \frac{k_2}{k_1}(E) \tag{7}$$

From (5) and (7) $\tag{8}$

$$L = k_2 E \left(M - \frac{k_2}{k_1} E \right)$$

The instantaneous rate of change in the population is a function of the size of the population. Landings are a function of both fishing effort and the size of the population, but population is also functionally related to fishing effort. Equations (4) and (5)

---

[7] M. B. Schaefer, "Some Considerations of Population Dynamics and Economics in Relation to the Management of the Commercial Marine Fisheries," *Journal of the Fisheries Research Board of Canada*, XIV, No. 5 (September 1957), pp. 669–81.

[8] *Ibid.*, p. 673. P is the current population in numbers of fish.

17

specify the approximate form of f (P) and ϕ (P, E). In the equilibrium, then, k_2 $EP = k_1P(M - P)$; the catch is equal to the rate of natural increase. From (5) and (7),

$$L = k_2 \, E \, (M - \frac{k_2}{k_1} \, E).$$

The elements underlying the yield-effort relationship in this model, shown graphically in Figure 1, may be explained as follows. In equilibrium, additions to the weight (biomass) of a fish population available for exploitation from recruitment and growth of individual fish are exactly offset by natural mortality. As fishing effort increases from level zero, a positive yield, increasing at a decreasing rate, can be sustained over some range. The reduction in population size and average weight per fish is more than offset by the reduction in loss to natural mortality and the increased rate of growth. Eventually, population effects dominate and further increases in fishing effort will actually reduce the sustained yield that may be taken. Marginal effects of both sets of factors are equated at the point of maximum sustained physical yield, with a smaller population of smaller fish, but with aggregate weight growing faster than in a free state. This "thinning" may, of course, introduce a host of further biological com-

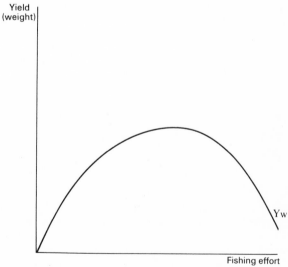

Fig. 1. Yield-effort function: standard gear.

18

plexities—for example, increased growth rates of other species as pressures on food supplies are reduced or substitution among competitive users of the food supply by species not exploited commercially—but the essential relationships are those indicated.

In discussing the application of the concept of diminishing returns to sea fisheries, Marshall did not clearly distinguish the effects of the change in scale, i.e., the decline in size of the so-called "fixed factor,"[9] with increasing rates of exploitation. Diminishing returns, in the classical sense, may contribute to the decline in landings as the number of fishing units increases and creates congestion in given fishing areas (a situation not uncommon in the salmon fisheries). In general, however, the monotonic decline in the rate of increase of yield with increased effort reflects primarily the inverse functional relationship between the size of the stock and the variable inputs—the scale effect.

Yield functions of this general type underlie virtually all present conservation regulations. Of themselves they imply nothing as to levels of effort and yield that will be reached or should be reached. They simply present, with greater or lesser accuracy, equilibrium values of the range of physical production alternatives available, given different sets of technical coefficients of production.

Over time, however, there has been a nearly universal tendency to equate "maximum" with "optimum" and to set maximum sustained physical yield as a primary objective. It has been rather generally (though not universally) assumed by fishery biologists that if we do not harvest all the fish that are available for harvest, we are wasting fish. This leads directly to the concept of the maximum physical yield (all the fish that are available in the long run) as an optimum or policy goal. We will return to this point again, but it is important to assert that the maximum physical yield is optimal only in a very special sense, not commonly spelled out in the literature. Society may specify that any quantity of fish is an optimum quantity; but in the absence of any such specification (i.e., the creation of an alternative social

[9] This point is elaborated in H. Scott Gordon, "On a Misinterpretation of the Law of Diminishing Returns in Marshall's *Principles*," *Canadian Journal of Economics and Political Science*, XVIII, No. 1 (February 1952), p. 96.

goal), *the optimal rate and method of fishing is that which maximizes the net economic yield from the resource.*

Finally, we should note that all these yield functions are partial. They apply to particular species of organisms. Any species lives, however, in a complex environment. The total yield from the environment—or, in economic terminology, the aggregate supply function—is a concept of great importance even if at present it is beyond meaningful quantification. An illustration of these interrelations is provided by the Pacific anchoveta. These fish provide the food for the marine birds that live along the coasts of Peru and Chile. Originally, only the guano produced by the birds was harvested. More recently, Peru has become one of the leading fishing nations of the world by bypassing the guano-producing birds and harvesting the fish directly and using them for fish meal. The aggregate supply function is thus some measure of the total protein production that is possible from this particular marine environment.

A great deal of progress has been made in converting these static yield functions to dynamic models, in which the time path of adjustment to changes in parameters can be studied analytically and empirically; but extraordinarily difficult data problems have limited application of these techniques to a few specific species. While the need for such intertemporal information appears much less urgent if the objective of regulation is solely to maximize physical yields than if maximization of the present value of net economic yield is the governing criterion, it is not trivial in any case; and since Pacific salmon populations, as indicated below, are continuously adjusting to complex short-run disequilibrating factors, the development of dynamic models assumes much greater importance in management of the resource.

OTHER BIOLOGICAL YIELD CURVES

Over time each year class of fish (recruits) becomes smaller in numbers, as disease, old age, and other mortality factors take their toll. Over the same time period, however, the weight of each surviving individual increases along a sigmoid growth path. At some point in time, the aggregate weight of the initial group of recruits will be at a maximum; i.e., the instantaneous rate of increase through growth will be equal to the instantaneous rate of decrease through mortality.

If it were possible to devise a fishing method sufficiently selective to take only fish in the size range corresponding to the ages at which the biomass is greatest, and if the gear actually contacted fish over the relevant range of sizes, the catch would approach that weight asymptotically at an infinitely large fishing effort (Figure 2).

Expressed in other terms, the use of partially or completely non-selective fishing gear inevitably catches some fish too soon; they would grow more than enough to offset non-fishing mortality if their capture were deferred. Indeed, for many pelagic (open water-dwelling) and demersal (bottom-dwelling) sea fish, biological overfishing is primarily a matter of catching new recruits before they reach a desirable size. Similarly, the larger fish taken are the remnant of a group which should have been taken earlier, since the subsequent weight increment does not offset the loss to other predators, disease, and old age. The high-seas fishery for Pacific salmon is an illustration of an operation that takes large quantities of fish which, left to return to spawning rivers, would

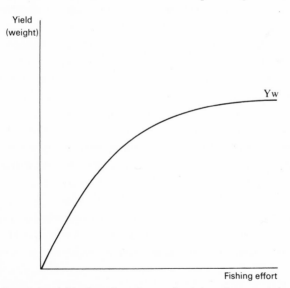

Fig. 2. Eumetric yield-effort function: selectivity of gear optimized at each level of effort.

21

probably gain substantially in net harvestable weight with relatively small marginal loss to natural mortality, though there is as yet no empirical verification of this point.

The ramifications of these interrelationships among effort, selectivity of equipment, and population size and composition are highly significant in many fisheries. If the selectivity of the gear can be varied to reject fish below the critical size, and if the gear actually contacts fish of the relevant size range, there need be no maximum in the yield-effort function. For each level of fishing effort there will be an optimum type of gear in terms of minimum size selectivity. As the level of fishing effort increases, the gear must be adjusted to catch larger fish, since mortality other than fishing will be minimized as fishing intensity increases. As indicated, the total yield approaches as a limit the maximum biomass (total weight) of each year class.

This asymptotic or eumetric production function is not general, however, since it requires conditions that are somewhat restrictive. It assumes, first, that a fishing method is (or can be) used which permits selection of the age (size) at which fish are first subject to capture; second, the population fished must be distributed in such a way that the gear actually contacts a range of sizes which includes optimal sizes, and the fishing must not be carried on at a level that affects recruitment significantly. Finally, in the common case in which the fishery exploits more than one population, adjustment of gear selectivity for each level of effort must normally represent a compromise. These qualifications rule out practical application of the eumetric concept to some important fisheries. Nevertheless, the concept of eumetric fishing is a significant contribution. It offers the possibility of sharply expanded output per unit of effort in the important trawl (and, possibly, seine) fisheries, where most of the essential requirements are met. More important, it has made even clearer the bankruptcy of maximum sustained physical yield as a normative concept in fishery exploitation and management, since this can be realized only with infinite effort (and infinite expense).

YIELD-EFFORT FUNCTIONS FOR PACIFIC SALMON

The general shape of the yield-effort function for all varieties of salmon will show the same characteristic hump indicated in

Figure 1, but for entirely different physical reasons. For demersal and pelagic species, the number of fish entering the exploited age-size group is believed to be independent of the existing size of the population over relevant ranges. The decline in the rate of growth of the catch with increasing effort reflects the effect of the fishery on the average size of the individual fish. In most demersal and many pelagic fisheries, a relatively wide range of age groups is actually exposed to the fishing gear.

The anadromous Pacific salmon, on the other hand, are available only for a short period of time; usually only one or two year classes will actually be exploited in a given season;[10] and the fish die after one spawning run. In the case of the salmon, the recruitment factor is, therefore, of paramount importance. The key relation determining long-run yield-effort functions is that between the spawners in year t and returning adult fish from that year class in the subsequent cycle year $t + i$. The length of the period i varies, depending on the species involved, from two to six years, and may also show some variation, in discrete annual units of time, for a single species. Bristol Bay sockeye, for example, may return after two or three years in the sea; and the migrants may, under some circumstances, remain either two or three years in a fresh water lake environment (one year as an egg, and one or two as fish).

The nature of the spawner-recruit relationship is anything but simple. It is obviously possible to reduce fish available for harvest in period $t + i$ to zero by catching all potential spawners in period t. What is less obvious is the empirically demonstrable fact that excessive escapement in t will actually result in a smaller number of returning fish (and perhaps fish of smaller unit size) in the following cycle year, as a result of overcrowding on the spawning beds, competition for food, and other density-dependent effects. Following Ricker,[11] the general form of the yield-effort relationship is indicated in Figure 3. Returning fish in $t + i$ are plotted against spawners in year t. The 45 degree line from the origin traces out a path of recruitment equal to escapement; i.e.,

---

[10] The troll fishery is an exception, and a high-seas net fishery might operate on several year classes.

[11] W. E. Ricker, *Handbook of Computations for Biological Statistics of Fish Populations*, Bulletin 119, Fisheries Research Board of Canada, 1958.

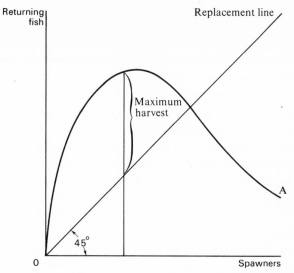

Fig. 3. Spawner-recruit relation: Pacific salmon.

for numbers of fish above the line, the distance between the 45 degree line and the total number of returning fish indicates the number of fish that can be cropped in each cycle year while providing replacement equivalent to that of the parent brood. The yield-effort relation, in physical terms, can be derived by taking the positive differences between the 45 degree line and the function OA.

There is thus general agreement that the number of recruits entering the fishery at time $t + i$ is a function of the number that escape to spawn at time t. Following an exposition by Paulik[12] let us designate escapement as E, returnees as N, and the proportion harvested in any year as U. Then $E_t = (1 - U) N$. The critical relation, still open to debate on both theoretical and empirical grounds, is that linking N_{t+i} and E_t. Paulik describes a series of "compensatory mortality" models of the form $N_{t+i} = cE_t g(E_t)$ where c is a constant related to the reproductive ability of the stock and $g(E)$ is a decreasing function of E representing the depressing effect of population density on productivity of

[12] For a detailed discussion, see G. J. Paulik and J. W. Greenough, "Management Analysis for a Salmon Resource System," Chapter IX in *Systems Analysis Ecology*, K. E. F. Watt (ed.) (New York: Academic Press, 1966).

the stock in an environment of fixed size. Variations in the assumptions as to *g* produce a number of alternative models, including those of Schaefer, Ricker, and Beverton and Holt.

For purposes of this study it is unnecessary to detail fully the complications introduced by the varying forms assigned to *g*. Suffice it to say that it is possible to produce a variety of time paths of adjustment to exploitation including both stable and damped oscillations. From our standpoint, the important points to be noted are: (1) the enormous complication of the problems of managed harvesting with very long adjustment periods involved for each separate salmon population; (2) the inevitable intermingling of many populations exploited by the same fishery; and (3) the tremendous variances around central values, both calculated and forecast. The functional relationships exist, but they are anything but stable, and the host of things that may happen to salmon during the fresh water, estuarial, and open ocean phases of the life cycle produce extremely difficult forecasting problems.

It is apparent that a maximum occurs in Figure 3, but the reasons for the configuration are entirely different from those underlying the function relating the yield of demersal or pelagic species to fishing effort. It will be recalled that the hump in the long-run yield function for demersal species results from a monotonic decline in the average weight of individual fish with increasing effort, since recruitment is largely independent of the size of the population over relevant ranges. In the case of the Pacific salmon, however, all returning fish in a given year will be from one or two year classes, each of identical age and very similar weight. The decline in yield at high rates of exploitation reflects a decrease in the number of fish available for spawning. The size of fish may be related to fishing effort, but possibly in a reverse manner; i.e., excessive escapement could conceivably result in slower growth, though there is no scientific evidence one way or the other.

In summary, the relation between spawning fish and the number of returnees available in the next cycle year for replacement and harvest is likely to be of the form indicated or, in the case of some salmon stocks, of the asymptotic type. The stability of

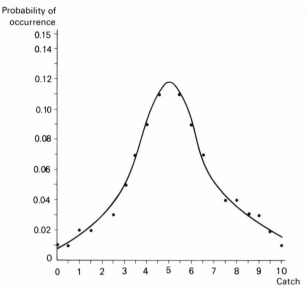

Fig. 4. Hypothetical catch probabilities: Pacific salmon.

the function for any one cycle period and the relative weight of this functional relationship as compared to non-density-dependent variables influencing the number of returning fish in any cycle year, are quite another matter. Figure 4 indicates the type of probability distribution of possible runs in $t + i$ for a given escapement in t with values not atypical of actual cases.[13] It will be noted that the range from low to high reflects a factor of ten: a range that is reflected in the unfortunate regularity with which forecasts differ strikingly from actual runs.

Dispersions around expected values also vary considerably by species. For example, variations are likely to be considerably smaller in the case of sockeye salmon, for which the one- or two-year period in a lake environment provides a buffer, cushioning variations in other non-population-density parameters. For pink salmon, on the other hand, variations will be much wider, since this species is much more vulnerable to extreme water conditions

[13] The distribution may well be log normal rather than normal and the curve would then be skewed.

during the critical period of egg fertilization and hatching.[14] For all species, however, the variances are extremely wide, and the yield-function is necessarily much less stable than that for most demersal species. The reason is obvious: the number of fish available for harvest in any given year from a given race is made up of one or at most two year classes, whereas a demersal fishery normally operates on a wide spread of age groups, most of which are relatively sedentary in habitat.

As in the more general model, the relations portrayed graphically in Figure 3 and Figure 4 are much simpler than those with which the salmon management program would normally have to work. These functions, as drawn, relate to an individual biological unit. Yet in virtually every case a salmon fishery will operate on more than one species and more than one semi-separate race of each individual species. Some degree of selectivity in harvesting, by species and by sub-groups of the same species, can be achieved, but only in limited degree. Moreover, any selectivity introduced into the fishery in an effort to harvest separate races as individual units inevitably raises extremely difficult problems as to the impact of such regulation on both costs and revenues. In fact, then, the yield-function facing a fishing fleet and a regulatory agency managing its activities is likely to be more jagged in shape than that portrayed in Figure 3, reflecting the fact that yields and efforts relate to a number of biologically distinct units. It also follows that the actual yield from a given level of effort will almost certainly be below the maximum that could be realized if each sub-group could be exploited optimally in a physical sense.[15] The choice of the level of information and forecasting accuracy becomes essentially a matter of balancing incremental costs of improving the level and predictability of

[14] For example, the 1963 catch and escapement of Puget Sound pink salmon was the largest of record. Returns in the corresponding cycle year, 1965, were the smallest of record. Excessive escapement in 1963 may also have been a factor in the poor yield of 1965.

[15] The problem has been stated and a maximum yield routine developed in G. W. Paulik, A. S. Hourston, and P. A. Larkin, "Exploitation of Multiple Stocks by a Common Fishery," *Journal of the Fisheries Research Board of Canada*, Vol. 24, 1967, pp. 2527–37.

catches against the reduction in inputs and increase in output achieved.

It is also important to stress that greatest physical yield from a managed salmon fishery is obtained by allowing the appropriate *absolute* escapement regardless of the size of the run. Hence, greatest physical yield over time would be systematically associated with greatest variability of year-to-year catch. The economic implications of the relation are discussed in Chapter 9.

Since the fishery for Pacific salmon is discontinuous, both the industry and any regulatory authority are also concerned with intraseasonal yield-effort relations; i.e., the catch per unit of time over the finite period in which a finite block of fish are moving through the gear operating along the migration path. This will depend not only on migration routes, rate of movement, and the intensity and location of fishing effort, but also on the behavior of spawning fish during the run. Pinks, for example, may "mill" in terminal fishing areas near the home streams for some time, with a few fish trickling into various spawning streams. Sockeye, on the other hand, are more likely to move continuously through the fishing areas in "blocks" destined for particular river-lake systems.

ECONOMIC FUNCTIONS

None of the biological models discussed purports to show the actual level of effort and catch to be expected under commercial exploitation (though, oddly enough, it is widely believed that they can show what effort and catch *should* be). If our model is to have any operational significance, physical yield must be converted to dollar revenue, and fishing effort to dollar cost.[16] For the sake of simplicity, assume that the elasticity of demand for fish over the relevant range is greater than unity, and that cost functions are linear; i.e., expansion of fishing effort simply means duplication of existing units without changes in factor prices. The resulting total revenue and total cost functions for the industry are superimposed on the physical functions in Figure 5.

[16] For an alternative approach to the following argument, see Crutchfield and Zellner, *op. cit.*, chapters 2 and 3, and Appendix 1.

28

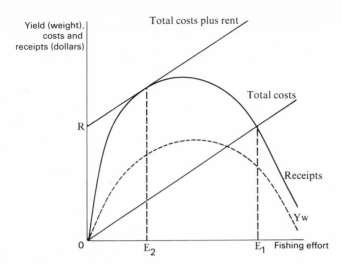

Fig. 5. Yield, receipts, and costs as functions of fishing effort (biological overfishing case).

Costs include a profit to the operator sufficient to induce reinvestment in equipment.

At the levels indicated, it is apparent that under conditions of free entry fishing effort will be pushed beyond the point of maximum physical yield. Equilibrium of a sort will be established only when total revenue and total cost are equated (OE_1); and, in the case illustrated, this is in the region of negative marginal physical yield. Average costs and prices are equated but marginal costs are clearly greater than marginal revenue.

Such an outcome obviously could not occur if the fishery were under private ownership. Whether he exploited the fishery himself or leased his rights, the private owner would take account of the potential rent that is available, since he is able to account fully, in the present, for the discounted value of future yield. On the assumption, first, that he must choose one among the several long-run or steady-state yields available to him, economic maximization would simply involve the determination of the level of effort—OE_2 in Figure 5—that would yield the maximum rent attributable to the resource (OR). At this level, marginal costs and revenues—to society, as well as to the private operator— are equated. This would yield the largest present value of the

29

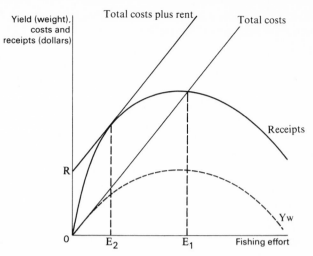

Fig. 6. Yield, receipts, and costs as functions of fishing effort (maximum physical yield case).

stream of net benefits available regardless of the discount rate applied to future income.

In the absence of ownership of the fishery and the restraining influence of inputs or explicit rent, severe overfishing in both biological and economic senses is apparent whenever cost-price ratios are very favorable. It is equally apparent that the situation is not self-correcting. Only in the extreme case where variable factors are costless would the fishery be exploited by a private owner at the level of maximum sustained physical yield.

In Figure 6, the cost function has been drawn to indicate a level of factor costs such that equilibrium is reached, with open entry, at maximum physical yield. If the fishery were privately owned, the output OE_2 that maximizes the net economic yield— that which equates marginal revenue and cost—would be chosen; and, as the functions are drawn, it would be less than the maximum physical yield, a condition that those not familiar with economic reasoning find disturbing. Even Schaefer, whose own analysis leads inevitably to the conclusion above, argues:

It would seem, therefore, that there is adequate reason to give first priority to maximizing the yield of the sea fisheries. This choice has been the basis of fishery management, in general, in the United States, and has, as noted by Graham (1956), been explicit in all the recent international conventions, in the New World. He also stated, that in the Old World there has not, as yet, been made any explicit choice among the possible qualities of the fishery. The conclusions of the recent United Nations Conference on the Conservation of the Living Resources of the Sea . . . indicates, however, that all the nations in attendance are giving high priority to this alternative.[17]

Part of this uneasiness stems from the instability of the optimal economic level of effort and catch. If we start with the total revenue and cost functions of Figure 6, OE_2, the level of effort that maximizes net economic yield, is below OE_1, at which physical yield would be greatest. Assume now an increase in demand and a rise of 25 percent in the price of fish. The upward movement in the revenue function will attract new entry if the fishery is unrestricted. The increase in revenue would generate additional effort and output would actually decline. If output were held at the level of maximum yield by regulation, new entry would simply raise costs until $TC = TR$ at OE_1 on the higher revenue function (i.e., total *effective* effort would be held constant, either by reducing the fishing time of individual units or their efficiency; the cost of the constant effective effort would rise in either case).

Under private ownership, the effect of the price increase would be an expansion of both effort and catch until *marginal* revenue and cost are again equated. Any increase in price will push the total revenue function upward in such a way that the level of effort which maximizes the present value of the net economic yield will be driven closer to the level which maximizes total physical yield; but it must remain lower as long as associated factor costs are positive.

To an administrator with no firmly ingrained concept of opportunity cost (i.e., the value of other production forgone by use of productive factors in fishing) and plagued by perpetually inadequate data, a definition of optimal catch and effort that fails to yield all the fish that are physically available (and that changes with every change in prices or costs) is likely to seem an invitation to chaos. Furthermore, if the fishery is shared by nationals

---

[17] Schaefer, *op. cit.*, p. 680.

of countries with different consumer preferences and relative factor costs, his discomfort may indeed become acute, since no single level of effort would be optimal for all participants.

It is impossible to quantify, without detailed knowledge of the shape of the relevant revenue and cost functions for each species, the difference between the optimum economic output and the maximum physical yield. The difference may be relatively minor where costs of fishing are very low relative to the prices of the product. For some species, including salmon, the distinction may be significant. In any event, it is necessary both to assert the distinction and to insist on the primacy of the economic criterion as the basis for policy decisions. On the other hand, the economic cost of excessive output in this sense is likely to be negligible in comparison with the waste associated with excessive inputs at any level of output in the absence of any restriction on entry.[18]

OPEN ACCESS AND ECONOMIC PERFORMANCE: GENERAL CHARACTERISTICS

Biologists were drawn into analysis of commercial fisheries by the governments and commercial interests seeking solutions to urgent problems of declining yields. Economists were attracted by the evidence of persistently low and unstable incomes and the obvious, and in some cases overwhelming, economic waste in mature fisheries.

The economic analysis follows directly from the traditional exposition of the theory of the firm. As indicated above, for any resource which is not owned and where there are no barriers to entry, average rather than marginal social costs will be equated to price; infra-marginal rents will be dissipated by the creation of excess capacity. In a dynamic situation (assuming a secular in-

---

[18] Turvey, *op. cit.*, has approached the problem of optimization as follows: he has employed a eumetric yield function. From this function he derives the biological optimum and the level of effort that maximizes the net economic yield. When both conditions are met, then the *optimum optimorum* is achieved. A second best solution is to achieve either one of the two suboptimum positions. For a criticism which asserts the asymmetrical nature of the two suboptima developed by Turvey, see G. Pontecorvo, "Optimization and Taxation, The Case of an Open Access Resource, The Fishery," in *Conservation, Taxation and the Public Interest in Extractive Resources*, M. Gaffney (ed.) (Madison: University of Wisconsin Press, 1966).

crease in national income, an income elasticity greater than zero, and a supply function less than perfectly elastic), more and more intensive rent will be dissipated, and more and more excess capacity will appear in the industry. In the fisheries, quasi-rents associated with individual skill and talents would remain; but "conservation" measures generally include regulations designed to penalize efficiency, which tends to eliminate some of the differences in skills. To the extent that this occurs, the "big catches" will be randomly distributed, a fact which tends toward further restriction on mobility in an industry already characterized by a tendency to "trap" ethnic or social groups not readily assimilated elsewhere in the economy.

In the fisheries, the peculiar nature of the supply function compounds this problem. Whenever fishing effort is carried to the point of maximum physical yield (or to the limit of a quota imposed by a regulatory commission), the supply function becomes backward bending or perfectly inelastic. At this point, which has been reached in many fisheries, an increase in demand raises prices and attracts entry. But the addition to capacity adds nothing to output. The existing or reduced output is simply shared among an increased number of inputs; i.e., the average cost curves of the individual producers slide up the inelastic (or negatively sloped) supply function. Competitive equilibrium is restored when all the rent is dissipated through additional entry. If, over time, the demand for fish products increases, more and more inputs are used to catch the same number of fish.

We have argued that excess capacity arises in response to the creation of economic rent which appears to entrepreneurs as excess profits in the industry. In the face of the existence of considerable chronic excess capacity, the industry becomes extremely vulnerable to any decline in the price of fish, the size of the catch, or both. With restricted factor mobility to leave the industry, the pressure of excess capacity, plus a fall in price and/or an autonomous decline in catch can result in economic hardship that is widespread and, for social reasons, extremely persistent.

The situation is intensified by the tenuous (and to the individual fisherman unknown) relation between current effort and future yields. The bio-economic models sketched above indicate equilibrium with factor incomes at opportunity levels. The economic waste is in terms of other output forgone as a result of excessive inputs. In most fisheries, however, imperfect knowledge results in an inherent tendency to "overshoot" the long-run equilibrium values. The resulting additional overcapacity, coupled with the asymmetrical entry and exit conditions, is largely responsible for factor returns well below opportunity levels—a situation common in mature fisheries. Considerable confusion has arisen as a result of failure to make explicit the fact that adequate factor earnings are no guarantee against excessive inputs.

The intense competition for a stable or shrinking supply of fish in the face of secularly rising demand obviously makes regulation more difficult. Since no one owns the fish, each man struggles for his share, a contest that encourages violations of regulations and poaching in all forms. More important, the obvious incentive for owners of existing gear to see that no one gains an advantage by improved efficiency generates constant pressure to reduce efficiency and to discourage technological change. Existing national and international agreements operating, tacitly or explicitly, on the concept of maximum physical yield are led to place restrictions on total output but not inputs. Since they cannot adjust the number of inputs, they "solve" the problem by a reduction in productivity of the inputs in an almost endless variety of ways, with an equally wide range of "explanations" for each.

The argument presented above suggests a revision in the usual classification of market structures. The competitive case contains a sub-group, the open access resource industries. These industries tend toward long-run competitive equilibrium but earn no economic rents. These conditions, free entry and open access, imply a systematic tendency for the malallocation of resources, which takes the form of excess capacity. In the case of the fisheries, this excess capacity, which results from the inability to "own" the resource and the structure of the industry, poses a constant threat to regulations imposed solely for biological purposes and provides the basis for a strong institutional bias against technological efficiency.

Thus far we have ignored the welfare problem involved in the distribution of the rent that could be made available under ideal allocation. Regardless of how these rents are distributed, however, welfare will be improved if they are captured either by individual entrepreneurs or by the state through taxation or license fees.

It is dangerous to generalize about a set of industries as diverse as the world's fisheries, but there is enough similarity among many of the major fisheries to permit some guarded statements about structure and some tentative hypotheses about the implications of that structure. At the level of the primary producer we usually find atomistic sellers facing oligopsonistic buyers. The seller's problem is generally compounded by the perishable nature of his product and his inability—financial, technological, or both—to provide storage capacity. Additional problems may arise from the seasonal nature of production and from violent fluctuations in output over time. The latter are biological in origin, but in most cases the amplitude of fluctuations in output is increased by man's own predation and, in the case of salmon, the need to assure adequate escapement from each run, regardless of its size. The instability of the production function provides the primary explanation of the peculiar share system of labor payment in most fisheries; under this system, the individual worker becomes a co-venturer with the vessel owner: an institutional arrangement rooted in need, but tending over time to act as a further deterrent to more capital intensive techniques.

Among different fisheries, conditions vary so widely on the buying side that only a few essentially deductive observations will be advanced. A monopsonist would impose a rational solution on the fishery; i.e., he would capture the rent by offering sellers a price that would permit only the most efficient exploitation of the resource to take place, and the malallocation of resources, which results from the combination of free entry and common property, would be avoided. If, in turn, the product market in which he sells is highly competitive, monopsony could provide a near-optimal level of output and real costs. The monopsonist would impose a price that would yield competitive returns to fishermen only if factor combinations and total inputs were optimal. Monopsony might, however, involve exploitation of the immobility of fishermen and hence a transfer of real income from fishermen to consumers (if the product market is atomistic).

Even though in many fisheries the degree of buyer concentration is high, the results to be expected from monopsony or effective collusive oligopsony are rarely observable. In fact, quite the contrary is the case. For example, in both the Pacific salmon fishery and the Pacific halibut fishery there is and has been relatively high concentration among the buyers of raw fish. But, instead of a tendency toward rational exploitation, these fisheries have become more and more overcapitalized. The increased capacity in the salmon fishery has been largely financed by the canners and processors as part of the competitive scramble for a share of the declining supply. This and similar evidence from other fisheries strongly suggest that even though there may be high concentration among fish buyers and processors, the structure is usually unstable. The primary reason is the absence of effective barriers to entry, a condition which derives from the relatively small size of producers, the geographical dispersion of landings, the technological conditions of processing, and the seasonal nature of operations.

The instability of the production function and the highly seasonal nature of the operation have other important implications for resource allocation in the buying and processing sectors. Short seasons create additional overhead costs in storage and marketing. In fact, the entire marketing organization tends to be affected by the underutilization of capacity. Under monopsony or factor monopoly, this would be minimized. But under unstable oligopsony or competition, the variability of yields, the technological conditions of production and the seasonal problem combine to encourage some excess capacity here as well as among the primary producers.[19]

[19] For examples of these effects in another fishery, see Crutchfield and Zellner, *op. cit.*, pp. 42–49. Their impact on performance of the salmon industry is discussed in subsequent chapters.

CHAPTER 3

Salmon Fishing Gear and
Methods of Regulation

~~~~~~

We present in this chapter a brief description of the types of gear employed in the Pacific Coast salmon fisheries and of the methods of reducing fishing mortality that have been used at one time or another by the regulatory agencies discussed in this study. With respect to the regulations, the mechanics of the various control measures are discussed, together with a brief analysis of the ways in which each is used.

SALMON FISHING GEAR

Trolling Equipment

Trolled lines are used to take chinook, coho, some pink salmon and a few sockeye from San Francisco to Alaska. Trolling is done from relatively small boats, usually manned by one or two men, using four to eight lines weighted to fish at different depths. Both natural bait and artificial lures are used, and virtually all trollers are now equipped to retrieve hooked fish rapidly with power gurdies. Despite its obvious inefficiency, trolling has grown tremendously in importance during the last decade. The prices of fresh and frozen chinook and coho salmon have been very attractive since World War II, and only the trollers clean and ice fish immediately after capture and thus preserve the quality required for sale in these markets. There is no reason, of course, why fish taken in nets could not be handled in ways that would provide fish of the requisite quality, but the financial incentive to do so has been lacking in most areas.

Unfortunately, trolling is a highly destructive fishing method, since it is essentially non-selective and captures or injures many immature fish. Even those large enough to be marketable would have gained far more than enough in weight to offset losses to natural mortality if allowed to reach full maturity. Those below legal size[1] must be shaken off the hooks and returned to the water, and survival rates are believed to be relatively low (particularly when fish are striking well and the fisherman is less disposed to be careful). Trollers operate on feeding grounds where fish can be taken prior to their spawning runs, and therefore take fish from many parent streams. Since it is difficult and expensive to even partially differentiate stocks in the trolling areas, biological management of any stock heavily exploited by the troll fishery is extraordinarily difficult.

Traps

The fish trap is a floating or fixed device positioned across the migration paths of salmon on their spawning runs and designed to lead salmon into a holding section from which escape is virtually impossible. The trap can be opened to permit escapement as desired, and can be used to hold fish for a short period of time before processing. Capital costs for traps are relatively high, but the cost per pound of fish caught is much lower than could be achieved by any other combination of gear in areas for which the trap is well adapted. It has been suggested that a relatively small number of strategically located traps could harvest the majority of Pacific salmon. These characteristics of the traps led to a series of increasingly bitter conflicts that dominated the course of salmon conservation in the entire Northwest. In Alaska, the controversy reached such proportions that it became a crucial determinant of

[1] At present—26 inches for chinook, 22 inches for coho, and 16 inches for pink salmon.

both the political and economic arguments for statehood. The traps were legislated out of existence in Puget Sound by 1935 and in Alaska in 1959 (with the exception of a few traps operated by the Metlakatla Indians).

Nets

Two types of net—the purse seine and the gill net—now account for the bulk of the salmon catch in all Pacific Coast areas except California (where only trolling is permitted). The purse seine is an enclosing or round haul net, set in a circle by the main vessel, with one end attached to shore or held by a skiff, and then pursed at the bottom to prevent fish from escaping as the net is retrieved. The net is then hauled aboard, over a drum, or with a davit or boom-mounted power block, and the fish are brailed aboard the vessel. The purse seine is a highly effective type of gear if the fish can be found congregated or "schooled up."

The gill net, as the name implies, is essentially a tangling device, usually fished across migration paths from a drifting boat. It is an extremely simple device, and can be handled by one or two men from small boats in a wide variety of environments. It is most effective, of course, when fish of relatively uniform size are running, since the size range over which a given mesh size is most effective is quite small. The gill net is usually fished at night. Highly efficient, monofilament nylon gill nets that overcome the daylight visibility problem have been developed in recent years, but their use has been prohibited in all fishing areas on the Pacific Coast.

Alaska prohibits the use of any vessel over 50 feet registered length (keel length) or 58 feet overall length (with the exception of vessels that fished for salmon with seines in Alaska prior to January 1, 1962 as 50-foot official registered length vessels). Except as restricted by regulation, all of the purse seiners fishing in both Alaskan and Puget Sound waters are seagoing vessels capable of fishing anywhere in the Pacific Northwest. Gill netters are typically much smaller, ranging from 26 to 40 feet, but they can and will move rapidly within regional fishing areas in response to shifts in the location of fish during the season.

39

The reef net is a type of gear peculiar to Puget Sound. It consists of a lift net suspended between two boats anchored over a shallow area in a salmon migration path. Observers mounted on a platform on the supporting boats can see salmon passing by and the net is lifted when sufficient numbers of fish can be taken. Properly placed, the reef net is an exceptionally cheap and efficient catching device; and, since it permits fish to be iced immediately, with relatively little damage from the net itself, it produces fish of unusually good quality. Good reef net locations are limited in number, however, and they account for only a small proportion of the Puget Sound catch.

Other types of nets fished from the shore are used in a few places in Alaska, but the types of gear discussed above account for virtually all of the commercial catch.

METHODS OF REGULATION

Fishery regulations can be divided into three major categories: selectivity controls that affect the size and/or the age at which fish can be taken; controls affecting the aggregate sweep efficiency of the gear employed; and fixed quotas. All of these, except quotas, are used extensively in the salmon fisheries of Alaska and Puget Sound. Quotas are used to limit catches in a few areas in Alaska (Yukon and Kuskokwim districts), and the method of allocating a variable total catch among Canadian and American fishermen in the Puget Sound sockeye and pink salmon fisheries might be considered a quota of a special type. A brief explanation of these techniques as they are used in the salmon fishery will obviate repeated explanations in subsequent chapters.

Selectivity Controls

Selectivity controls may be of two types. A minimum mesh size for either purse seine or reef net will permit fish below a certain size to escape (not necessarily without injury), while retaining all individuals above that size. The gill net, on the other hand, will reject fish both smaller and larger than those in the critical range. Within this range the net will trap fish by the gills or fins. The selection is not a black and white proposition, however. One can construct (and there have been constructed) net selection curves which show the relative efficiency with which different sizes of fish are caught. As used in the salmon fishery, specification of mesh size is used primarily as a method of concentrating fishing effort on particular species rather than on different age groups. Minimum mesh sizes for purse seines, for example, enable them to take chum and pink salmon in areas where immature chinook and coho salmon are also concentrated, without much damage to the latter. Since the salmon involved are significantly different in size, a fairly high degree of selective fishing for the desired species can be achieved. The selectivity of the gill net can be used to permit harvesting of one species of salmon while avoiding capture of others as long as the size differences of the individuals in the respective groups are large enough to place the undesired species outside the effective catching range of the net. Neither type of net can be made perfectly selective in the desired range, of course, but the degree of control is sufficiently high to allow management of separate species of salmon as separable units, and thus permits a much greater total yield than if completely non-selective nets were used.

It is apparent that selectivity controls can be, and all too often are, used to reduce the efficiency of the fishing unit by the simple expedient of requiring mesh sizes either too large or too small for the specific populations fished. It should also be noted that gill nets selectively fish certain age segments of particular stocks. In the Skeena River, for example, the current mesh size selectively removes five-year-old fish at one and one-half times the rate of four-year-olds. Current research also suggests the possibility of increasing the yield from a salmon stock that regularly generates a surplus of males, which are significantly different in size from the females, by altering the mesh size appropriately.

Control of Fishing Capacity

Most of the regulatory methods employed in the Pacific salmon fishery are of types that affect the catching power of the fleet as a whole. The most obvious method of accomplishing a reduction would be, of course, to reduce the number of fishing units. This has never been attempted directly in the Pacific Coast salmon fishery, though legislation to this effect has been proposed on more than one occasion in both Washington and Alaska. It was accomplished in an indirect fashion in Bristol Bay by establishing an alternative number of fishing days depending on the number of units of gear fished.

The most general of the techniques actually employed to reduce aggregate catch has been the time closure. In the Pacific salmon fishery, where each class is available only once, and only for a short period of time, control over fishing periods can be made an effective and flexible instrument to control total fishing mortality. Things can become complex, however. The fish are only available in one season, but often to a sequence of fisheries. Many of the time closures are as much concerned with a politic diversion of catch as with regulating harvest. General closures— usually covering the winter months—have been used to minimize fishing pressure on chinook and coho stocks exploited primarily by the troll fishery.

Much more important, however, control over fishing time provides flexibility and an absolutely essential safety valve. For example, it can be used to afford protection to immature fish, particularly if it is coupled with area closures and restrictions on winter fishing. Intraseasonal closures are the principal means of exercising selective control of fishing effort on specific species and on sub-groups within a given species, provided the timing of the runs varies enough (and provided that identification of the separate groups is possible). As indicated in Chapter 8, judicious use of weekly closures permits the International Pacific Salmon Fisheries Commission to exercise some measure of individual control over identifiable segments of the Fraser River sockeye runs.

In the rather special case of the sockeye and pink fishery of Puget Sound, in which equal division of the catch between American and Canadian fishermen is required under a bilateral treaty, time closures permit the Commission to equalize the catch while maintaining effective control over total escapement.[2]

Above all, the power to close the fishery completely is essential where speed and drastic curtailment of fishing effort on short

[2] This is not necessarily desirable, of course; see the analysis of the treaty and the ramifications of the equal catch requirement in Chapters 8 and 9.

notice are required. As indicated in Chapter 2, salmon runs are so erratic in size and timing that precise forecasting, though theoretically possible, is certainly not within our grasp at present, and a standby control of absolute effectiveness is essential.

In the setting of the Pacific salmon operation, area closures are a complementary rather than competing technique. The biological characteristics of the Pacific salmon make them peculiarly vulnerable to excessive fishing effort in the estuaries of the spawning streams. Salmon frequently will not go up river when waters are low and clear. A freshet is required to move the fish, and when fish are milling in an estuary waiting for proper water conditions they can obviously be fished literally to the point of extinction. In some areas, notably the Fraser River, the area closure is also a highly useful technique for dealing with "blow backs"—a situation in which fish that have escaped the Strait of Georgia fishery turn back into open areas in association with certain wind and river conditions, and are again subject to capture.

In both instances, there may be other reasons for pushing fishing effort away from the mouths of the streams. The quality of many races of salmon begins to deteriorate as soon as they reach estuarial waters; and, up to a point, better average quality can be realized by taking fish further from the river mouth. In the absence of detailed knowledge of the sub-groups that make up a given run, forcing the fishery outside might provide some more balanced harvesting than is likely if the fishery were carried on in the immediate vicinity of the estuaries, without effective separation of stocks for management purposes. This is only conjecture, however; it has never been rigorously examined.

Area closures are also widely used to ameliorate conflicts between incompatible types of fishing gear. The need for this type of regulation in the salmon fishery has diminished in recent years with the elimination of fixed gear such as traps. Conflicts between purse seiners and gill netters and, increasingly, between commercial net fishermen and sport fishermen still give rise to external diseconomies that can be resolved in part by area limitations on the use of specific types of gear.

In one sense of the word, the general prohibition of high-seas net fishing for salmon, effective in all Canadian and American waters, might be viewed as an application of the area closure technique. Quite apart from the economic absurdity of a high-seas race for fish, most of which will later appear inshore, in compact groups, and in prime physical condition, closure of the high seas to commercial net fishermen is essential for any kind of selective biological management of salmon stocks. The situation in Puget Sound and British Columbia in the 1940's and early 1950's is a case in point. Canadian and American fishermen began a "leap-frog" process that threatened to carry the sockeye and pink salmon harvest into the Pacific Ocean, beyond the control of the International Pacific Salmon Commission, negating completely the concept of regulation based on the analysis of spawning requirements for all separable races of the Fraser River run.

It might be noted, parenthetically, that area closures are often a substitute for adequate research, management and enforcement. Where quality considerations permit, it might be much more efficient, for example, to permit harvesting in estuarial areas and even in some rivers; but in the absence of detailed knowledge of the stocks and rigid supervision of the operation, the danger of disastrous overfishing is so great that the area closure is the only feasible safeguard. With more than 2,000 major spawning streams in Alaska alone, the need for this type of regulation is apparent.

Limitations on the size of fish that can be taken have been enforced in the Pacific Coast salmon fisheries for decades. As indicated above, the limits are presently set at 26, 22, and 16 inches for chinook, coho, and pink salmon respectively. These size limits apply almost entirely to the troll fishery since all types of salmon nets are used almost exclusively on mature fish during or just before the spawning run. The usefulness of size limits is debatable. On the one hand, they do serve to discourage fishing in closed areas where large numbers of immature fish might otherwise be taken. On the other hand, the size limits have never been set at levels that would restrict the troll catch to fully mature fish. They do not prevent the inherent waste that results when the non-selective troll gear takes fish one or two years before maturity, despite strong evidence that increments in growth continue to exceed losses from natural mortality until maturity is

44

reached. In addition, undersized fish returned to the water have relatively low survival rates. It is true, however, that the minimum size limits tend to push trollers away from areas where large numbers of immatures are mixed with larger fish because of the delay involved in shaking off undersized fish and rebaiting the lines.

The size limit has operated usefully in one special case—the sport fishery inside Puget Sound. Until the late 1950's when a 16-inch limit was imposed, salt water anglers took extremely large numbers of immature coho, which are highly vulnerable to several types of sport fishing gear during the period when their size ranges from 12 to 15 inches. Since natural mortality of these fish thereafter is relatively low, "investment" in future growth is highly desirable from the standpoint of both commercial and sport fishermen.

All the types of regulation discussed above are essentially efficiency-reducing techniques from the economic standpoint. They could hardly be otherwise, since all of them involve either limitations on fishing time or area redistribution of fishing effort, both designed to reduce the total catch taken with a given number of operating units. Unless men and gear could be switched without delay to other occupations within the fishing season, some economic cost is inevitably imposed on the industry by all the controls discussed above. The only exception would be selectivity controls that restrict the catch of immature fish. In this case, a rough kind of investment decision is involved. Although no specific attention is directed toward costs, virtually all selectivity techniques that defer capture of Pacific salmon until maturity probably involve an increase in gross weight and in the discounted value of the catch net of increased losses to other predators and disease.

Limitations on Vessels and Equipment

In addition to the regulations described above, there is an almost endless series of limitations on fishing equipment and vessels; most of these limitations are deliberately designed to reduce technical efficiency of the individual operating units. In Alaska, as already noted, it is required that no salmon-fishing

45

vessel be over 50 feet in registered length.[3] Whether this reduces pressures on the resource is open to considerable question, but it cannot be denied that it has produced some extraordinary changes in vessel design in order to cram 70 feet of equipment into a 50-foot hull. The mere fact that such a regulation was written is *prima facie* evidence that a vessel larger than 50 feet would be more efficient, at least in some areas. As in so many regulations of this type, the real purpose of the limitation had nothing to do with conservation; it was simply a device to keep the larger Puget Sound purse seiners out of the Alaska fishery.

All of the common types of nets used in salmon fishing are restricted in various ways that limit efficiency, whether by accident or by design. These include the specification of mesh sizes larger or smaller than those that would be optimal for the species exploited, restrictions on the length and depth of nets, and restrictions on the materials that can be used in nets (in particular, the prohibition against use of monofilament nylon in the manufacture of gill nets). Above all, the elimination of the trap must be considered in efficiency-reducing method, since one of the avowed purposes of the action was to provide more employment in the fishery, particularly for local residents.

The need to reduce the aggregate efficiency of the salmon fleets, in the absence of any authority to control the number of units, has extended into the area of auxiliary equipment as well. Salmon fishermen are forbidden, for example, to use electronic fish-finding gear, though its applicability—particularly for purse-seining operations—has been established. Commercial fishermen are also forbidden to use aircraft or helicopters for fish-spotting— apparently because the rather confined waters in which salmon schools run prior to and during their final spawning would make such techniques very effective despite the high operating costs of the aircraft. Perhaps the crowning restriction was the insistence until the 1950's that Bristol Bay gill-netters use sail instead of power.

Details of the economic impact of the various regulations discussed in this chapter are illustrated by reference to the Alaska

---

[3] With some exceptions mentioned on page 39.

and Puget Sound segments of the fishery in subsequent chapters. It should also be stressed, however, that the development of regulatory programs in both Alaska and Washington was most certainly an exercise in political pressure rather than political economy. A prominent fishery scientist, after reviewing the history of Alaska regulations, concluded that few of them bear any relationship to conservation in either physical or economic meanings of the word.[4] To a far greater degree, they represent the net impact of power plays by one group or another: fisherman versus processor; gill netter versus purse seiner; mobile gear operator versus trap owner; and so on *ad infinitum*. If the resulting pattern of regulation amounted to no more than a series of transfer mechanisms we would be less concerned about it. But, as subsequent chapters make clear, the failure to consider economic objectives in the regulatory programs and the consequent failure to consider economic costs as a basis for appraising one type of control over another left no consistent basis for selection of methods to reduce fishing mortality. In the absence of such criteria, it is hardly surprising that the choice of regulatory methods became even more a matter of pressure and politics. The ultimate sufferers were both the salmon and the men concerned with their production and consumption.

[4] William F. Royce, "Prospects for Alaska Salmon," speech at Fourth Annual State Convention, Alaska Chamber of Commerce, Juneau, October 15, 1963. Issued as Fishery Circular No. 203, University of Washington, Seattle, Washington.

CHAPTER 4

The Alaska Salmon Fishery:
The Environment, the Attitudes

~~~~~~

There is a haunting quality that runs through the written history of the Alaskan salmon fishery. From the early reports to the United States Fish Commission, in 1889 by Tarleton Bean and in 1899 by Jefferson Moser, through the analyses of Gilbert and O'Malley in 1919, Rich and Ball in the 1920's, Gregory and Barnes in the late 1930's, George Rogers in the 1960's, and Richard Cooley in 1961, there is evidence of a constant preoccupation with the threat and, in some areas, the fact of the destruction of the resource.[1]

The seeds of destruction have been ascribed in varying degree by different authors to the peculiar vulnerability of anadromous fish; the shortsightedness and greed of man in general and of absentee interests in particular; and the ineptitude of the federal bureaucracy. The following is typical of the criticisms inspired

[1] The extensive literature provides an excellent description of the fishery. Since much of it is readily available and since the emphasis in this study is on the economic effects of regulation, only the descriptive material relevant to our theme is cited directly.

by the evident abuses and economic waste underlying the depletion of the resource:

> This frank declaration [by the Bureau of Commercial Fisheries] that
> the management philosophy was based upon the interests of non-
> resident investors rather than on local factors (which presumably would
> include the salmon as well as the Alaskan fishermen) should provide
> the final explanation of the paradox of a conservation agency failing
> to provide research or adequate management until too late.[2]

No one should deny or underestimate the influence of the
shortsighted, and at times irresponsible, competitive tactics of
some segments of the industry or the ambivalent and, until less
than a decade before the end of its stewardship, generally unsatisfactory administration of the resource by the federal government. Nevertheless, the partial truths in the various assertions
about the causes of the ills of the Alaska salmon fishery do not
add up to an adequate explanation. As Adam Smith noted, personal gain is the basic motivating force in a private enterprise
economy; and there are too many cases of resource-oriented industries in which economic performance is reasonably good to
ascribe the salmon industry's woes solely to the greed of the
non-resident canners and the unwillingness or inability of the
federal government to regulate human predators effectively.

Two positions can be distinguished among the groups dis-
tressed over the state of the salmon fishery. For some, the prime
concern was the impact on the general welfare of the American
people of the heedless depletion of a valuable part of our
national heritage. For others, the primary concern was and is
the economic development of the state of Alaska. To the latter
group the external forces operating on both government and

[2] George W. Rogers, *Alaska in Transition: The Southeast Region* (Baltimore: The Johns Hopkins Press, 1960), p. 311. See also Richard A. Cooley,
Politics and Conservation: The Decline of the Alaska Salmon (New York:
Harper & Row, 1963). Cooley's analysis of the ills of the fishery is much
broader than Rogers'. His study, like Rogers' works, stresses the political
aspects. His exhaustive research carefully spells out the long history of congressional neglect and bureaucratic ineptitude. However, he goes beyond this
position and provides, for the first time in the literature on this fishery,
recognition of the complex economic problems implicit in the exploitation of
an open access resource with easy entry conditions.

49

industry seemed to inspire methods of resource exploitation in-
consistent with optimal long-run utilization of the salmon and,
therefore, with the sustained economic growth and development
of Alaska. The word "therefore" is crucial. In some cases there
appears to be an uncritical tendency to equate optimal utilization of the fishery resource with maximum regional development.
In others, there is more than a casual implication that if the two
should conflict—if, for example, the national interest and the
Alaskan interest were not served identically by any given fishery
policy—the latter should take precedence. The argument for
working from the welfare of Alaska toward the national welfare
is vital to an understanding of the development of the salmon
program, since it embodies the attitude of the territory, and now
the state, toward regulatory problems and objectives involving
all national resources. The Alaskan position is particularly well
articulated by Rogers:

> In order to understand the more unique characteristics of the state-
> hood movement and its aftermath—those aspects in which it differed
> from as well as resembled the traditional colonial pattern of develop-
> ment into political independence—it will be necessary to study the
> process by which political institutions and organizations have evolved
> in Alaska.
> The process of elaboration of government coupled with the more
> traditional colonial attitudes toward political and economic relation-
> ships produced a widely held philosophy: if the political structure is
> changed to approximate that found in a mature economy and society,
> the structure and size of the economic and social base will automatically
> expand and adapt to that normally found with the corresponding
> political structure. "Political structures are the fundamental determinant
> of economic forms and conditions." If Marx had produced his theory
> of economic determinism by standing Hegel on his head, why not
> create a theory of political determinism by standing Marx on his head?[3]

Three elements—the behavior of the industry, the role of
government, and the attitudes of the resident population—
clearly contributed to the decline of the fishery, but they were
not, individually or collectively, the primary cause. The real
source of the difficulty, as indicated in Chapter 2, lay in unre-

---

[3] George W. Rogers, *The Future of Alaska: Economic Consequences of
Statehood* (Baltimore: The Johns Hopkins Press, 1962), p. 148.

stricted access to the resource. Coupled with the elements mentioned above, open access guaranteed fulfillment of Michael Graham's classic dictum that "all free fisheries are doomed to failure." None of the alternative policy suggestions of those espousing the "greed-stupidity-colonialism" explanations would, in the long run, have altered the process of overexploitation and economic decline of the industry in any significant way, though the identity of the gainers and losers might have been different.

Several other conditions peculiar to the resource and the environment have compounded the difficulties of the Alaskan salmon fishery. The anadromous nature of the fish makes them more vulnerable to overfishing than most marine species, since they can be taken in areas and at times when they are densely concentrated. Indeed, as noted in Chapter 2, the salmon is one of the few marine fish that can literally be exterminated by a commercial fishery. The high value of the catch relative to production costs and the rising secular trend in salmon prices have maintained, except for brief periods (after World War I, and in the early 1930's), the economic incentive for exploitation at a high level. The geographic dispersion and isolation of the fishery have greatly increased the administrative difficulties of regulation. Finally, the remote location of the fishery has prevented direct observation of developments in the fishery by the general public and so has minimized the influence of public opinion on the behavior of both industry and the regulatory agencies.

THE ENVIRONMENT

The geographical dimensions of the Alaskan salmon fishery are overwhelming. It extends over 2,000 miles along the entire coast from southeast Alaska to the Bering Sea, and in time the commercial fishery will probably extend even farther north to the Arctic Ocean. (The Japanese are, in fact, already operating there.)

Straight line distances (see Map 1) give only a slight indication of the dispersion of fishing and processing effort. The Alexander archipelago in southeast Alaska contains over 1,000 islands; many are large, with deep bays and coves, and almost all contribute to the fishery. To the westward, salmon are taken from Yakutat, through Prince William Sound, Cook Inlet, around Kodiak Island, along the Alaskan peninsula, and in Bristol Bay.

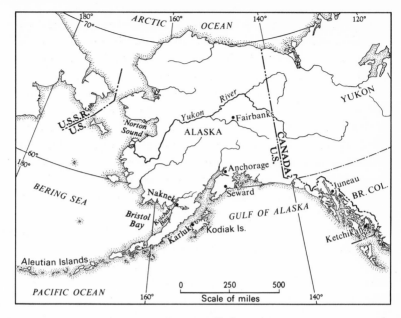

Map 1. Alaska

All five species of salmon[4] are found in Alaska in commercial quantities, though their relative importance varies considerably by area. The life cycles of the several species vary in detail, but they share two characteristics that are significant in terms of regulation and utilization. All die after spawning once, and all spend a substantial part of their lives in the open ocean, where observation and measurement are extraordinarily difficult.

For canning, the sockeye, chinook, coho, pink, and chum salmon normally rank in that order in terms of unit value. Only the chinook and coho salmon enter the fresh and frozen market in quantity, though pinks and chums are occasionally used to plug seasonal gaps in supply. The Pacific salmon deteriorate rapidly once they are caught, and must be processed quickly if their initial high quality is to be maintained in any prepared form.

In the absence of any regulation, the most effective unit of

4 I.e., sockeye, chinook, coho, pink, and chum. As indicated in Chapter 2, the use of the term "red" for the sockeye is so common in Alaska that it is used in Chapters 4 through 7.

salmon fishing gear, in the short run, was a barricade erected across a stream. Apart from this self-defeating technique, all the basic types of equipment described in Chapter 3 have been employed in Alaska.[5] In recent decades, regulations and the scarcity of fish have virtually eliminated all gear other than purse seines, gill nets and trolled lines.

Originally, red salmon, and subsequently the reds and pinks, have accounted for the bulk of the commercial catch in Alaska. The most valuable fishery for reds has been in Bristol Bay and in western Alaska, while the bulk of the catch of pinks has come from southeast and central Alaska. In recent years the wide fluctuations in catch associated with the overall decline in the fishery have caused yearly shifts in the geographical pattern of landings. For example, 1960 was a particularly bad year in southeast Alaska, and therefore central Alaska accounted for 75 percent of the landings of pinks. In an average year, however, southeast Alaska produces over half the pinks landed in the state. Chums and the limited number of cohoes used for canning are taken primarily in southeast and central Alaska, while chinooks and cohoes for the frozen and mild-cure markets are harvested in southeast Alaska, virtually all by trollers.

The geography of the fishery has been a vital factor in the development of the structure and organization of the salmon canning industry. Throughout its history the salmon fishery has been isolated from markets, labor supply, service facilities, and the flow of information required for efficient productive activity. In recent years the growth of Alaska's population and improvements in transportation have reduced, but not eliminated, the dominant influence of distance. It is now possible for the cannery or the fishing vessel in need of emergency repairs to get spare parts and assistance much faster, but the centers of fishing activity in Alaska are still difficult areas in which to operate complex equipment.

The impact of distance and isolation on industrial organization is increased by the short length of the season. In Bristol Bay, for example, fishing for sockeye may be limited to less than two

[5] Richard A. Cooley, *op. cit.*, gives a detailed description of the gear employed in specific areas in Alaska.

weeks, and usually does not extend over five weeks. (A smaller fishery for pinks in even-numbered years and for early chinooks may extend over a period of two months.) Into this brief period must be packed the full productive activity that will cover the costs of transportation and quartering of fishermen and shore workers, installation and maintenance of capital equipment, processing, storage, and financing. Within the season, virtually all costs except fish purchases are essentially fixed costs, and most marketing costs are incurred after the pack is completed.

In the past the location of processing units has been based on the local availability of fish. The canneries could reach out only a very limited distance for raw materials of acceptable quality. Time is vital in transporting, holding and processing any type of fish, and salmon are very vulnerable to deterioration after capture. In southeast Alaska, where the supply comes from many small and widely scattered sources, the perishability problem encouraged the growth of smaller processing units. In other places, such as Bristol Bay, where the sources of supply are more concentrated geographically, a different structure of processing firms emerged, with larger units and more frequent opportunities for consolidation of operations.

Throughout Alaska, entry into the canning field has remained relatively easy, since the simple technology of canning made it possible in all but a few locations to achieve an efficient scale of operation with a small investment in readily available equipment. In addition, the canning companies and marketing factors contributed to easing the effects of credit rationing on new entrants. More recently, the development of brine tanks, improved freezing methods, and the increased use of tenders have extended the range of the individual canneries and thereby tended to increase their size. But since this has taken place during the period of general decline in the availability of fish, the implications of these changes on economies of scale and the organizational structure of the industry are not clear.

THE LABOR FORCE

Gold, not fish, was responsible for the Territory's initial boom; between 1890 and 1910 the population of the Territory jumped

54

from 32,000 to 64,000 persons, 25,000 of whom were natives (i.e., non-white). After 1910 the population declined, then slowly recovered, until in 1939 it stood at 73,000, of whom 32,000 were natives. The population upsurge created an Alaskan work force initially composed largely of whites but it gradually absorbed elements of the native population as they came into the labor market. Both white and native Alaskans were discriminated against at first, and in some instances were completely excluded from the labor agreements in the fishing industry negotiated outside the Territory.[6]

The necessity of drawing a seasonal labor force from outside Alaska has had serious political as well as economic consequences. At first there was no choice. The numbers, geographic distribution, and composition of the resident population simply could not provide the necessary work force for fishing or plant operations. The bulk of the labor employed was recruited in Seattle and San Francisco. Alaskans were not a party to either the formulation or resolution of the issues that arose as the industry's labor force took form and eventually moved into union organizations.

The struggle by Alaskans to gain an equal footing in "their" fishery contributed heavily to the political attitudes that developed in the Territory and eventually made the control of the fisheries a key issue in the drive for statehood. The years of discrimination and political frustration led Alaskans to articulate the question of control of the fisheries on a straight "we-they" basis that left little room for rational discussion of the biological and economic complexities of the resource and the industry. The path of development of the Alaskan salmon fishery might have been different had control been vested earlier in the hands of resident Alaskans, but there is no reason to believe that it would have come much closer to maximizing the potential net economic yield of the resource. In fact, since the state assumed jurisdiction of the fisheries in 1959, the number of fishermen and vessels on Bristol Bay has more than doubled.

---

[6] *Ibid.*, p. 52. Cooley points out that in certain areas Alaskans were actually prevented from fishing.

The Dimensions of Failure

Before proceeding further with the analysis of biological and economic constraints on the industry, it is necessary to establish clearly the nature and significance of the failure to use the Alaskan salmon stocks effectively. No observer of the fishery can deny that the shortcomings of performance were massive, and that they were both biological and economic.

Millions of dollars are wasted today in catching a fraction of the fish that were formerly available. Details of the decline in catch and of the resulting economic waste are developed in subsequent chapters. But subsequent refinements in analysis can

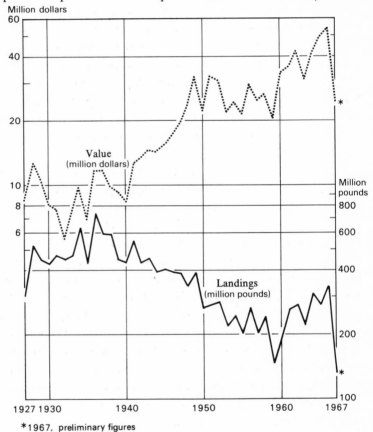

*1967, preliminary figures

Fig. 7. Total Alaska salmon catch (pounds and value), 1927–67.
Source: Table A-1.

only expand upon the melancholy facts that are obvious in the following charts. Figure 7 shows the trend in physical output and value of the catch from 1927 through 1967. It should be kept in mind that the data in this chart are aggregative for both biological species and geographic areas. Sharp movements in the series (particularly in a downward direction) reflect, therefore, a general collapse in physical availability. The high point in the fishery was in 1936 when over 700 million pounds were landed. In recent years the fishery has operated at approximately 40 to 45 percent of the average for the peak five-year period 1934–38. The protracted nature of the decline after 1936 is suggestive of the magnitude of the task involved in restoration of the fishery; and it is not clear that the level of output in 1936 represented the maximum physical yield that could be realized.

The inverse relation of the landings and value series indicates a secular rise in prices over the period. As indicated in Figure 8, the prices of salmon actually rose more rapidly than the general price level. The implications of the persistent upward trend in real prices are best seen in Figures 9 and 10, however, in which

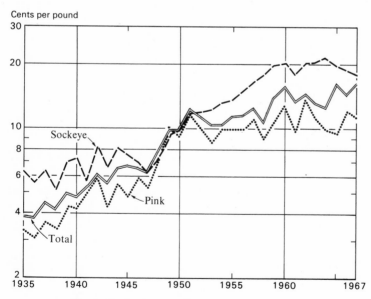

Fig. 8. Real prices of Alaska salmon, 1935–67.
Source: Table A-2.

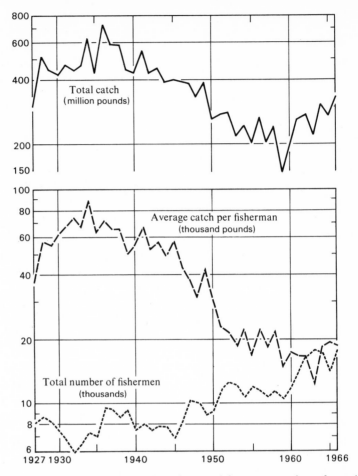

Fig. 9. Alaska salmon fishery (number of fishermen, total catch, and catch per fisherman, 1927–66). Source: Table A-3.

the ultimate absurdity of a consistent increase in fishermen and equipment in the face of a declining catch emerges. In the early 1930's the average catch per fisherman was over 70,000 pounds. Today the average catch per fisherman is only slightly over 15,000 pounds.[7]

[7] In one sense these figures are distorted by the inclusion of trap-caught fish in the earlier periods. But they do reflect, as they should, the physical impact of enforced elimination of this most efficient type of gear. A full evaluation must, of course, take account of the cost of capital and labor inputs and their relative weights in different types of gear.

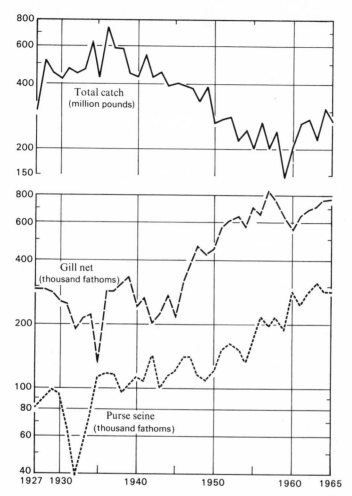

Fig. 10. Alaska salmon fishery (fathoms of purse seine and gill net, and total catch, 1927–65). Source: Tables A-1 and A-4.

In spite of the catastrophic decline in physical yields, the value of the catch per fisherman has kept pace with consumer price levels, so that the fishermen have continued to earn opportunity incomes, albeit with wide fluctuations from year to year and with wide variations among fishermen in any one year. In addition, there has been a change in the ethnic composition of the fishermen. Over the years more non-white Alaskans have entered the fishery and, for a number of reasons, this group has a lower

59

opportunity income than fishermen recruited in Seattle and San Francisco.

The facts just cited summarize the gross measures of developments that cannot be regarded as sensible in economic or technological terms. Today, twice as many fishermen, using more capital equipment, are employed in catching about 40 percent as many fish as were taken in the mid-1930's; and, parenthetically, the fish are no more difficult to catch in the 1960's than in the 1930's—quite the contrary.

The typical human reaction is to look for simple remedies for obvious problems. Unfortunately, as the biological data on the salmon accumulated, it became obvious that the underlying population dynamics were extremely complicated. It has become equally clear that the simple solutions so often advanced to solve the ills of the fishery were, in the light of our growing knowledge of the resource, only simple-minded.

BIOLOGICAL CONSTRAINTS ON REGULATION[8]

The first step in developing a sound biological basis for regulation is the identification of the various unique biological units (or races of fish) in the fishery. There are approximately 2,000 salmon streams in Alaska. In each of these there is at least one species of salmon; in many, there are several; and in some, all five species are found. In addition, through the fishing season, which extends from late spring into early fall, a stream may contain more than one sub-group of the same species. For example, stream A may have a run of pinks and one of chums. In addition, the same stream may have an early run of sockeye and a late run of sockeye, each of which is a distinct biological unit, with separate characteristics and a different set of conditions

---

[8] We are heavily indebted to Dr. William F. Royce, Director, and other members of the staff of the Fisheries Research Institute of the University of Washington for much of the material in this section. For a succinct summary, see W. F. Royce, "Concepts and Practices in the Conservation of Fishery Resources," in *The Fisheries: Problems in Resource Management*, J. A. Crutchfield (ed.) (Seattle: University of Washington Press, 1965), pp. 19–22. An excellent example of the complications involved in actual management processes can be found in W. F. Royce, "Pink Salmon Fluctuations in Alaska," in *Symposium on Pink Salmon, H. R. MacMillan Lectures in Fisheries, 1960* (Vancouver: University of British Columbia, 1962), pp. 15–33.

necessary for survival and reproduction. These four units are not completely independent, however. They stand in close proximity to one another in time and space; they may compete for living and spawning areas and food supply; and they may even prey upon each other. The current estimate is that there are approximately 10,000 biological units, defined in these terms, in the Alaskan fishery, with relatively little genetic interchange among them. We have barely touched the edges of the biological knowledge necessary to make even crude estimates of the factors determining the productivity of these units.

A further distinction must be made between biological and management units. The latter may be defined to include all salmon that "enter a distinct fishing area during a specific period, and must be regulated as a unit. From the standpoint of efficiency, each management group should be as small and include as few spawning groups as possible."[9]

The problem is further complicated as one moves away from the rivers and streams themselves into the river mouths, estuaries, bays, and offshore migration routes. In these open territories, many of them prime fishing grounds, salmon from many different river systems will be intermingled, and identification of fish from any particular management unit is extremely difficult.

Viewed in this light, the failure to lay a solid biological groundwork for the regulation of the Alaska salmon fishery is less an indictment of the agencies involved than of nature's perversity in setting up such a complex problem. Intelligent biological management of populations as complex and diverse as the Pacific salmon could not be developed in a decade or two even under far more favorable conditions than ever actually prevailed in Alaska. But it could have proceeded at a much more rapid pace were it not for the preoccupation with quack remedies and simple solutions.

GEOGRAPHIC EXPANSION OF THE FISHERY

Accurate assessment of the physical dimensions of the depletion problem in Alaska was made much more difficult by the dual

[9] Royce, "Concepts and Practices in the Conservation of Fishery Resources," *op. cit.*, pp. 21–22.

61

nature of the expansion of the fishery—geographically and in terms of the species exploited.[10] Examination of the literature on the Alaskan fishery clearly indicates this extension process. In its most generalized form it involved a shift from a red salmon fishery to a red, pink, and chum salmon fishery. Bean,[11] writing in 1889, notes that neither pink nor chum is used in canning, and Moser in his investigation of 1898 comments:

> As the redfish is the commercial fish, the other species being packed incidentally or to fill up quotas when other kinds are scarce, no attempt was made to examine streams other than those having the red salmon.[12]

Up to 1910 red salmon dominated the catch. Thereafter the pack of pinks and chums exceeded the pack of red salmon, and during the 1930's and 1940's the pack of pink salmon occupied the same dominant position the reds had held earlier. In the 1950's the wide swings in output associated in part with the declining fishery have made the relationship less consistent.[13]

The simple conclusion usually drawn from this evidence of extension of the fishery is that output over time was increased and sustained by exploitation of fresh stocks as the older ones became depleted by overfishing.[14] This hypothesis is usually ex-

[10] For a careful analysis of this process by a biologist see B. B. Parrish, "Problems Concerning the Population Dynamics of the Atlantic Herring with Special Reference to the North," in *The Exploitation of Natural Animal Populations*, E. D. LeCren and M. W. Holdgate (eds.) (New York: John Wiley and Sons, 1962), pp. 9 ff.

[11] Tarleton Bean, *Report on the Salmon and Salmon Rivers of Alaska*. Bulletin of the U.S. Fish Commission (Washington: U.S. Government Printing Office, 1889).

[12] Jefferson Moser, *The Salmon and the Salmon Fisheries of Alaska* (Washington: U.S. Government Printing Office, 1899).

[13] Cooley, *op. cit.*, pp. 66 ff., discusses in greater detail the changing composition of the catch by district. The entire process was a perfectly rational one from the standpoint of a competitive industry with unrestricted entry. In a rough way, the geographic expansion of operations involved a marginal balancing of higher catch rates against higher transportation and operating costs. Similarly, the shift to pinks and chums represented a trade-off of volume against unit price.

[14] This is the position taken by many other writers. For example, see Cooley, *op. cit.*, p. 69; Willis H. Rich and Edward M. Ball, *Statistical Review of Alaska Salmon Fisheries*, Bureau of Fisheries Document No. 1041 (Wash-

tended to include a corollary that in the earlier years of the fishery the size of the market, not the supply of fish, limited the catch. More recently, physical limits on supply and stricter regulations have been the primary determinant of the size of the catch. In general the industry can, except as a result of mischance such as bad weather, *catch* all the salmon legally available plus some additional but unknown quantity. However, the necessity of providing for the full season's operation in advance, based on forecasts that have occasionally proved inaccurate, resulted in catch limitations because canneries could not process all the fish received. Fishermen in the Kodiak area were "put on limits" in 1962 and 1964 because of inadequate cannery capacity, and the same situation occurred in 1965 in Bristol Bay.

The hypothesis and its corollary are consistent in a general way with the available evidence, but the biological data needed to indicate when, in which specific areas, and to what degree overfishing took place are not available. The overfishing question turns on the inadequacy of our information on natural mortality and population fluctuations. More particularly, data on natural mortality rates in the fresh water and ocean stages, and on the resiliency of individual stocks in the face of exploitation, are not adequate to permit construction of definitive dynamic population models. For this reason biologists cannot specify with certainty the timing and extent of overfishing in specific areas in the past. As we shall indicate below, there is substantial evidence of excessive exploitation in the early commercial fishery, but it is impossible to tell where, and to what degree, the damage to the stocks was self-correcting. Given this biological uncertainty about the fish populations, we are left with two important questions: Can the runs be rebuilt at all? And if so, by what techniques and at what cost?

Despite the biological and economic complexities, the physical environment in Alaska is basically favorable to some degree of

---

ington: U.S. Government Printing Office, 1928); C. H. Gilbert and Henry O'Malley, "Special Investigations of the Salmon Fishery in Central and Western Alaska," *Alaska Fishery and Fur-Seal Industries in 1919,* Bureau of Fisheries (Washington: U.S. Government Printing Office, 1920), pp. 144–45. Rogers, *Alaska in Transition,* p. 98.

restoration of the fishery, and indeed some may already have oc-curred. In Alaska, in sharp contrast to the rest of the United States (and, to a lesser extent, Canada), the environment of the fish stocks has not been altered perceptibly by dams, deforesta-tion, siltation, toxic and organic pollutants, and other by-products of urban civilization.[15] It appears that under careful biological regulation, the Alaskan fisheries could be rebuilt, if cost condi-tions warranted it, to a level of output well above the low point reached in the 1950's. If, in addition to careful biological man-agement of the stocks, the fishery were rationalized in an eco-nomic sense, further increases in physical catch and significant additions to *net* dollar revenues could be anticipated.

THE POLITICAL ENVIRONMENT

Unfortunately, there are many crosscurrents at work which may prevent even partial realization of these objectives. The ob-vious long-run problems are biological and economic, but the operational obstacle is the inability thus far to create a political environment that will permit the introduction of economic effi-ciency as a criterion for management. Until it is, the biological constraint, in purely physical terms, will remain tighter than it need be.

The Alaskan community is preoccupied with the problem of economic growth. The standard preconception in Alaska, as elsewhere, is that growth is defined primarily in terms of in-dustrialization. This position is supported in part by the poten-tial for hydroelectric power generation in Alaska.

Both the Bureau of Reclamation and the Corps of Engineers are intrigued by the power potential in Alaska, and their reports and investigations have kept public interest in those projects at a high level.[16] The most spectacular of these projects is at Ram-part on the Yukon River. A dam at this point would create a lake larger than Lake Erie with a power potential more than

[15] Various authors writing about Alaska's future place quite a different emphasis on the future of the fishery in terms of the growth of competing water users and polluters. Rogers, *The Future of Alaska*, esp. pp. 233 ff., is essentially concerned with tourism, oil and gas, and especially hydroelectric power development.

[16] George Rogers, *The Future of Alaska*, Chapters 2 and 7.

double that of Grand Coulee, and the Rampart site is but one of many. Without commenting on the merits of or possibilities for Alaskan power development, it is clear that the drive for urbanization and power development may pose a threat to the fisheries even before any other change in water quality or spawning areas could be expected.[17]

Theoretically, the development of hydroelectric power on a large scale would proceed only if benefits of the project exceed all costs, including fishery losses. Even so, for the reasons set forth in Chapter 2, under present conditions net benefits from the fisheries will tend toward zero. Until a more rational basis for management is instituted, conventional benefit-cost analysis will consistently undervalue the potential economic contribution of the fisheries. Given a period of rapid industrial development, the inadequacy of the current basis of valuation of benefits or losses to the fisheries from multiple-purpose river development projects constitutes a serious threat to the fishery.

The condition of the Alaskan economy further complicates the position of the fisheries *vis-à-vis* other economic objectives of the state. Alaska grew very rapidly during and after World War II. More recently, growth has been much slower.[18] In Alaska, as in other areas with redevelopment problems, the burden of adjustment will fall heavily on the work force—in this case a work force in which at least one component, the native, is especially immobile in an economic sense. In these circumstances, for political and humanitarian reasons, it will be extremely difficult to restrict entry to an occupation traditionally open. The temptation to view the fishery as a disguised but nevertheless crucial part of the state's unemployment compensation program is very strong.

CONCLUSIONS

The basic conclusion to be drawn is that there was no significant degree of conservation in the Alaska salmon fishery until

[17] The development of the logging industry in southeast Alaska and the oil and natural gas industry in the Kenai Peninsula are the industrial sectors of the Alaskan economy with the greatest growth prospects, and both are potentially capable of destructive effects on salmon habitat.

[18] Rogers, *The Future of Alaska, op. cit.*, p. 280.

the 1950's. There was no dearth of regulation; but to be effective, regulations must rest on the development, from relevant knowledge, of policies directed toward objectives that enhance human welfare, and they must be enforceable in the sense that they are acceptable to and adhered to voluntarily by a strong majority. It is highly doubtful that these conditions were met adequately until the 1950's.[19] Even today, while the necessary conditions for meaningful biological regulation are better understood, our ability to quantify the underlying biometric models and to devise simple and effective control techniques is limited to very few areas.

Thus, while biological knowledge of the salmon has increased rapidly, it is still far from adequate for satisfactory management of most of the Alaska salmon runs, even in a purely physical sense. As one would expect in such a heterogeneous fishery, the degree of scientific knowledge of the basic resource is highly uneven. In Bristol Bay, the combined efforts of federal and state governments and the Fisheries Research Institute of the University of Washington provide a basis for reasonably accurate forecasts of the runs. This is not true elsewhere in Alaska, although the accumulation of essential data is proceeding gradually. Despite substantial research effort by the United States, Canada, and Japan, our knowledge of the effects of the Japanese high-seas salmon fishery on Alaska stocks is still far from adequate in terms of the needed adjustment of American and Canadian regulation.

We defer until later a discussion of the economic implications of alternative concepts and techniques of regulation. At this point it is merely noted that only a few preliminary attempts have been made to relate regulation to desired economic effects. (The area registration procedure discussed below is an illustration.) But these have usually been described and justified as biological regulations. No program of regulation geared specifically and openly to economic objectives has been attempted in the fishery.

[19] Royce, "Pink Salmon Fluctuations in Alaska," *op. cit.*, documents this statement in convincing fashion. See also Howard Baltzo, "Enforcement of Alaska Fisheries Regulations," in *Biological and Economic Aspects of Fisheries Management*, J. A. Crutchfield (ed.) (Seattle: University of Washington Press, 1959), pp. 104–8.

The importance of regulating with at least some cognizance of economic efficiency as a goal is threefold: it raises the hope of lasting improvement in the net yield from the fishery; it makes biological regulations less onerous and more enforceable; and it usually gives another degree of freedom in a biological sense by reducing the constant threat posed by continuous excess fishing capacity.

On a strict interpretation of this argument, it could be argued that there is no meaningful regulation of the Alaska salmon fishery today, since the efficiency of our regulatory measures, even in purely physical terms, is far from adequate in the light of current knowledge of stocks and of available control techniques. It is also true, however, that by the middle of the 1950's there was a sharp improvement in the effectiveness of the biological management of the fishery. The several aspects of regulatory activity were, for the first time, recognized explicitly, and significantly larger amounts of funds were made available to carry on the work.[20]

Three elements of the preceding discussion should be borne in mind in reading the history of salmon regulation in Alaska set forth in the following two chapters: (1) the persistent search for causes of depletion other than overfishing; (2) the recurrence of partial recognition of the key role played by the economic consequences of depletion and regulation; and (3) the thoroughness with which these insights were ignored in actual policy formation.

[20] Royce, "Pink Salmon Fluctuations in Alaska," *op. cit.*, p. 23.

CHAPTER 5

Development of the Alaska Salmon Fishery

THE PRE-COMMERCIAL FISHERY

The standard image of the pre-commercial Alaska salmon fishery is one of rivers teeming with salmon, with fishing effort limited to the native Indians, Eskimos, and bears: a picturesque tableau, with no visible threat to the stocks of fish. The impact of the bears remains indeterminate, but recent anthropological research has greatly revised the picture of Indian activity. In the process, it has begun the task of analysis of the links between pre-commercial subsistence fishing and the pattern of growth of the commercial fishery.[1]

Based upon per capita caloric intake, Hewes estimated total aboriginal consumption of salmon in Alaska at about 33.5 million pounds. This is over 15 percent of the 1960 catch. Consumption was by no means evenly distributed along the coast, however.

---

[1] See Gordon W. Hewes, "Aboriginal Use of Fishery Resources in Northwestern North America" (unpublished Ph.D. dissertation, University of California, Berkeley, 1947); and Richard A. Cooley, *Politics and Conservation: The Decline of the Alaska Salmon* (New York: Harper & Row, 1963), chapter 2.

In areas where the native populations were heavily concentrated, the proportion of the runs harvested was very high, and the intensity of the native fishery on some streams may have reached levels beyond those at which physical yields would be maximized.

There is also evidence that the native population was stable for a relatively long period. Population growth, even with an abundant food supply, was prevented by a number of natural checks, primarily infant mortality, tribal wars, and a high accident rate.[2] Local food shortages may have been important, especially at times and in places where salmon stocks were systematically overfished. There is no convincing evidence of waste in the utilization of the salmon.[3]

This was not true of the effect of aboriginal use on other animal populations such as caribou, reindeer, and walrus. These stocks were available only for short and unpredictable periods, and the tendency was to slaughter indiscriminately as many animals as possible while they were available. The salmon runs, regular and abundant, did not provide the excitement of the hunt, although they did provide the basis for many religious ceremonies. Regardless of how one interprets the implications of the fishing effort of the aboriginal people, there is considerable evidence, according to Hewes, that the Indian fishery was intensive enough to affect abundance in some localities where there was a heavy Indian population. (Precisely what it did to individual races of salmon in the sense discussed in the previous chapter is, of course, unknown.)

One possible explanation of the connection between the native and the commercial fishery asserts that a set of circumstances (primarily the impact of infectious diseases) sharply reduced the native population in the nineteenth century. The decline in fish-

[2] We are indebted to Professor Margaret Lantis for suggesting this explanation.

[3] This account places a different emphasis on the interrelation between the salmon and the native people than does Rogers, whose position is also adopted by Cooley. He suggests that a fine balance existed between the aboriginal population and the environment and that this balance reflected the gearing of the institutional organizations of the tribes to the resource base: the fishery. George W. Rogers, *Alaska in Transition: The Southeast Region* (Baltimore: The Johns Hopkins Press, 1960), p. 278.

ing effort permitted the stocks to recover at about the time the commercial fishery began.[4]

THE COMMERCIAL FISHERY: THE BEGINNING

Bean, in 1889, sounded the note of urgency that echoed continuously thereafter as investigator after investigator reviewed the state of the salmon resources:

> In my opinion this river will soon cease to show such a state of productiveness, if indeed it has not already done so, and we must conclude that the most formidable obstruction at present to the ascent of salmon in the Karluk for the purpose of reproduction is overfishing.[5]

The conditions described by Bean in his investigation of the red salmon fishery at Karluk were noted some ten years later by Moser. In discussing the law of 1896 Moser states:

> This law, like others that have preceded it, is generally regarded as inadequate in some vital respects by those having the interest of the salmon fisheries at heart; but there is little agreement among cannery people as to what the law should be. There is, however, a general inclination toward a tax on the output of each cannery and saltery for the support of hatcheries, and the suggestion that streams be leased for a term of years has everywhere met with favor.[6]

In his account of his journey along the coast Moser describes various methods of barricading streams and provides over 15

[4] This analysis is, at best, only reasonably satisfactory from a social and economic viewpoint. It is, of course, no more than an elementary *a priori* deduction concerning the biological status of the resources. In addition, the Indian population was concentrated in particular areas. Except for these settlements there was no systematic fishery. Moreover, the tendency to move the village to a new site if local salmon runs declined provided a mechanism for subsequent recovery of the stocks.

[5] Tarleton Bean, *Report on the Salmon and Salmon Rivers of Alaska.* Bulletin of the U.S. Fish Commission (Washington: U.S. Government Printing Office, 1889).

[6] Jefferson Moser, *The Salmon and the Salmon Fisheries of Alaska* (Washington: U.S. Government Printing Office, 1899). Moser's voyage took one summer. He was actually in Alaska less than three months, and his trip extended from southeast Alaska as far west as Dutch Harbor in the Aleutians. Examination of streams on foot was a time consuming, arduous process, and the large number of barricades he found in his limited investigation suggests that the practice was widespread.

In evaluating these comments by early observers of the fishery, keep in mind their ignorance of the biological complexity of the problem and therefore their lack of any real or workable concept of the appropriate yield from the resource.

pages of photographs of stream barriers, some so well constructed he could not remove them. These barricades were permanent and complete barriers to the passage of the fish upstream. Any fish in these streams that escaped the fishermen had to spawn below the barrier or not at all. In addition to permanent obstacles, many streams were virtually sealed off by nets across the mouth, by the use of leads for a trap, or by diverting channels. In the face of this kind of "fishing" one can only wonder how any fish survived. The extent of the damage to the various stocks is, of course, unknown. In some instances particular races may have been completely destroyed, or the environment altered in such a way as to make recovery of specific stocks impossible. On the other hand, once the more destructive practices were stopped, something approaching complete recovery probably took place in many streams.

A number of factors operated during the early period of the fishery to prevent complete extermination and also to conceal the extent of damage that did occur. The fishermen were primarily concerned with red salmon; any damage to other species was incidental to their main activity. The fishery was limited in time and space. Some early and late runs escaped the fishery, as did some of the runs that were either too small to be of interest or were located in inaccessible areas. Except where streams were completely barricaded, it was virtually impossible to take all the fish from any one run; hence, some spawning almost always took place. Aggregate statistics on the yield from different areas provide no answers to the effect of overfishing on particular races. But by the 1920's overfishing was sufficiently widespread to be generally apparent.

Does anyone doubt that the wonderful Karluk River has suffered impoverishment since the days when it was easily able to produce, year after year without interruption, packs of 150,000 to 200,000 cases of red salmon? A comparison of the early days with the average packs of the last years is convincing that, whether or not on the Karluk bad is now giving place to worse, the river is consistently on a lower level of production than formerly.[7]

[7] Willis H. Rich and Edward M. Ball, *Statistical Review of Alaska Salmon Fisheries,* Bureau of Fisheries Document No. 1041 (Washington: U.S. Government Printing Office, 1928).

Or, in more specific reference to the Nushagak fishery:

This is exactly the sort of thing that biologists have warned could be expected, the logical explanation being that the catch was held up, in spite of real depletion, by an increased intensity in fishing until finally the break came and severe depletion became apparent all at once.[8]

These writers were also deeply concerned about the intensity of the fishing effort. The period just before and especially during World War I was one of rapid expansion in the fishery—in 1914 there were 82 canneries in Alaska, and by 1918 there were 135. Gilbert and O'Malley estimated a one-third increase in gear from 1912 to 1919 in the Naknek-Kvichak district.[9] Their report infers that if the gear has increased but total output has not (i.e., if yield per unit of effort is falling), then there is overfishing.[10] However, inadequate evaluation of the effect of rising prices did not prevent this perceptive report from suggesting the need for major institutional reorganization of the fishery.

We have stated at length our conviction that the industry has now reached a critical period, in which the salmon supply of Alaska is threatened with virtual extinction, unless a radically new administrative policy be substituted for the one now in force.[11]

These observers clearly saw the competitive struggle for fish as the prime cause of the threat to the resource, and therefore suggested leasing of fishing sites or the creation of property rights in the fishery to conserve the fish.[12]

Both sets of authors also conclude that, as of the time of their writing, there was no effective regulation.

Further improvements can be made in the Alaskan field by making more adequate provision for the enforcement of the laws. Not only are

[8] *Ibid.*

[9] C. H. Gilbert and Henry O'Malley, "Special Investigation of the Salmon Fishery in Central and Western Alaska," *Alaska Fishery and Fur-Seal Industries in 1919.* Bureau of Fisheries (Washington: U.S. Government Printing Office, 1920), p. 150. Rich and Ball, *op. cit.*, p. 160.

[10] The arguments asserting overfishing advanced in the 1920's by these authors do not rely solely on the above deduction to support their position. They also point to increasing amplitude of fluctuations in the catch as evidence. Also see Rich and Ball, *op. cit.*, p. 43.

[11] Gilbert and O'Malley, *op. cit.*, p. 143.

[12] Gilbert and O'Malley, *op. cit.*, p. 143.

our fishery statutes now pitifully inadequate, but they are unusually and unnecessarily made difficult of enforcement.[13]

Up to 1922, then, it is safe to say that the catch of salmon had not been affected materially by legal restrictions.[14]

With respect to these observations, a word of caution is in order. It is deceptively easy, with the benefit of hindsight, to ascribe far more knowledge to these authors than is really appropriate. Nevertheless, it is desirable to avoid the tendency of some critics who lump the observations and recommendations of these authors with those of the emotional and fundamentally antiscientific conservation movement of the times.[15]

It must also be borne in mind that those who opposed what they regarded as the "wanton waste and destruction" were anything but a unified group with logically conceived objectives and policies.

Regulation may not have been meaningful in terms of economic efficiency, but it does not follow that the organization of the fishery and fishing practices were the same as they had been when described by Bean and Moser in the late nineteenth century. An extensive body of regulations had been established, and the United States government was committed to their enforcement. Streams were no longer barricaded, although practices nearly as destructive were certainly widespread.

Before the passage of the White Act in 1924 the biological basis for the development and enforcement of regulations was inadequate. What had emerged and matured, however, was the structure of the economic organization and technology of both the fishery and the processing-marketing operations. This structure and technology were modified only slightly in the period from the early 1920's to the advent of statehood; and it is in the interaction among the economic organization of the industry, the regulatory process, and the biological characteristics of the salmon stocks that the causes of the decline of the fishery must be sought.

13 Gilbert and O'Malley, *op. cit.*, p. 148.

14 Rich and Ball, *op. cit.*, p. 140.

15 For an excellent evaluation of this movement and its strange assortment of concepts, objectives, and bedfellows, see Harold Barnett and Chandler Morse, *Scarcity and Growth: The Economics of Natural Resource Availability* (Baltimore: The Johns Hopkins Press, 1963), chapter 3.

Furthermore, the Organic Act of 1912, which granted limited self-government to the Territory, contained many restrictive provisions not imposed on other territories, of which the most onerous to Alaskans was the retention of federal jurisdiction over the fisheries. Control of the fisheries quickly became a crucial political issue and eventually the rallying cry in the long battle for statehood. Since the canners had lobbied extensively for the restrictive amendments adopted by the Senate in 1912, these fishery amendments became the focus of the attack on "outside interests."[16] The resulting conflicts were hardly conducive to the development of a sound and workable management program.

INDUSTRIAL ORGANIZATION

In its initial stages the development of the Alaskan salmon fishery followed a pattern similar to that of many other industries in the period of rapid industrialization in the 1880's. There were at that time few limitations on supply, the technology of the canning industry was simple, and, with free entry, competition was intense. In 1888, there were 17 canneries in operation and they produced 412,000 cases of salmon—more than double the output of the year before. A year later, 37 canneries were in operation, and 714,000 cases were packed.

The market could not absorb this level of output at profitable prices and the industry moved toward rationalization through "trustification." This was facilitated by the already high degree of concentration in some segments of the industry and the centralization of its administration in San Francisco and Seattle. The solution adopted in 1893, after the failure of some preliminary loose-knit agreements, was to merge a number of firms into the Alaska Packers Association (APA). Each company received shares in the new organization in exchange for its canneries; all were obligated to buy additional shares to provide working capital; and no shares were sold to the public. The Association is still one of the leading firms in the industry. During the preceding period, under various loose-knit combinations, numerous canneries had been closed—22 in 1892 alone. Conse-

16 Ernest Gruening, *The State of Alaska* (New York: Random House, 1954), pp. 148–53. Cooley, *op. cit.*, chapter 5.

quently, there was no necessity for additional large-scale readjustments in capacity after 1893. By ordinary industrial standards these changes were relatively small. Most of the canneries were essentially hand production units, with very little machinery.

In 1894 the Association packed 72 percent of Alaska's salmon, and from 1893 to 1899 it dominated the fishery, producing—on the average—80 percent of the pack. Industry output increased slowly to almost a million cases by the end of the decade. From 1899 to 1902, largely under the leadership of APA, the industry began to develop the Bristol Bay fishery, and output expanded to an average of approximately 2.5 million cases per year. (This was approximately equal to the average pack in the late 1950's and early 1960's.) APA lost ground, however, during the period of expansion, and in 1901 accounted for only 46 percent of the pack. The next two producers, Northwestern Fisheries Company and North Alaskan Salmon Company, packed 13 percent and 7 percent respectively. APA, however, still occupied the dominant position in the fishery, packing over three times as many cases as its next largest competitor. At this time, the first four firms accounted for 70 percent and the first twelve, for 88 percent of total Alaskan output.

After 1910, rising prices induced another period of rapid expansion in the fishery. Output nearly doubled from 1910 to 1915, when almost 6.7 million cases were packed. This expansion was marked by considerable new entry, especially in southeast Alaska. By 1920, APA's share of an industry pack of 4.4 million cases had fallen to 13 percent. The first four firms packed 36 percent and the first twelve, 55 percent.

The earlier expansion had been based almost exclusively upon red salmon. Much of the growth after 1910 was achieved by extending the fishery to other species. Under the impetus of World War I, commercial exploitation of the chums—the lowest-priced salmon—began. The extension of canning operations to pinks and chums shifted the geographic center of the fishery away from western Alaska and was primarily responsible for the sharp drop in the concentration ratios. These ratios fluctuated markedly from year to year with changes in the geographic availability of fish, but over the 44-year period, extending to the present, they have been essentially stable. Although the overall degree of concentration declined, as indicated, this was due to changes that took place primarily in southeast Alaska. Concentration increased as one went north and west in Alaska, and this situation has persisted.

Concentration ratios are notoriously tricky measures of market control. In addition, high concentration ratios imply nothing with respect to control over prices except in conjunction with an explicit analysis of entry conditions and the degree to which individual firms are able to differentiate their products successfully.

The latter question can be disposed of summarily. Raw fish, by species, are homogeneous industrial inputs. In the salmon industry the only basis for differentiation would be quality and uniformity, a dimension easily translated into price differentials. Effective brand promotion of end products is only moderately important in the canning segment of U.S. industry, and is of little or no significance in the market for fresh and bulk frozen fish. It is increasing in importance, as would be expected, in the rapidly growing market for packaged and branded frozen salmon steaks and fillets.

With respect to concentration and entry conditions, a distinction must be drawn between the markets for end products and those for raw fish. Canned salmon is a relatively durable product, capable of extended storage with little quality deterioration and sold through conventional food marketing channels. All American production and imports from Canada and Japan are closely competitive in a market that is national in extent. Even frozen Alaska salmon are sold in every major city outside the south and southwest, again in competition with Canadian imports.

Buying markets for raw salmon, on the other hand, are narrowly circumscribed by the extreme perishability of the product, the high costs of transportation, and the geographic dispersion of the fishery. The discussion that follows makes it clear that oligopsony, rather than oligopoly, is the pivotal competitive relationship in explaining some of the most significant aberrations in performance of the Alaska salmon industry.

Data limitations make it virtually impossible to discuss concentration in either product markets or the markets for raw fish

Table 1. *Concentration Ratios: American Salmon Canners*

(*percent of total pack*)

Year	First four firms	First eight firms	First twelve firms	First twenty firms
1954	29	45	59	74
1955	30	49	62	79
1956	34	53	65	81
1957	32	50	62	76
1958	32	57	64	81
1959	40	58	71	85
1960	44	65	76	89
1961	39	60	70	84
1962	38	59	73	87
1963	44	64	77	87
1964	40	64	79	89
1965	50	71	80	89

Source: M. E. Rubinstein, "The History of Concentration in the Canned Salmon Industry of the United States" (unpublished Bachelor's thesis, Harvard University, 1966), Appendix A.

in the desired detail, but a general view of the level and trend of concentration in the product market from 1954 to 1965 is set forth in Table 1. For recent years it is possible to delineate major submarkets for raw fish with reasonable accuracy, and a summary of the current competitive structure in these areas is presented in Table 2.

Unfortunately, simple ratios do not give an adequate picture of concentration in the fishery. Control over the supply of fish has always been the crucial element in a stable, collusive oligopsony. The fish, once caught, cannot be inventoried.[17] The canneries traditionally were dependent on local supplies, and the key instrument in pre-empting local supply was the fish trap. Furthermore, the trap could, under certain circumstances, hold live fish for short periods and thereby smooth the flow of production through the cannery. The trap was also, under circumstances common to many areas in Alaska, the most efficient type of gear, a characteristic that added considerably to confusion in the regulatory process. In general, these traps were "cannery" traps, and

[17] In recent years the use of chilled brine has enabled packers to hold fish for a longer period before canning, but only at higher cost.

Table 2. Concentration Ratios: Alaska Salmon Canners, by Area

(*percent of area pack*)

Area	1954	1955	1956	1957	1958	1959	1960	1961	1962	1963	1964	1965
Central Alaska												
First four firms	42	46	38	36	42	59	51	52	47	62	45	60
First eight firms	67	70	63	71	69	81	73	77	72	82	74	82
Southeastern Alaska												
First four firms	41	42	44	43	42	45	48	38	44	50	50	46
First eight firms	65	63	68	66	65	73	70	63	66	75	81	78
Western Alaska												
First four firms	54	50	55	53	57	65	61	61	53	54	62	58
First eight firms	72	74	79	76	76	90	83	84	76	77	86	82

Source: Rubinstein, see Table 1.

even when they were independently owned they normally had working agreements with particular owners. This extension of ownership by the processor to gear was, of course, true in varying degree of all other fishing operations, particularly in more remote areas of Alaska.

Traps were rare in western Alaska (there were none in Bristol Bay). Their use was somewhat more widespread in central Alaska, but the majority were in the southeast. The share of the catch taken by traps increased steadily during the major periods of growth of the fishery. Prior to 1909 traps took less than a quarter of the landings. By the early 1920's this figure had grown to almost 45 percent and in the late 1920's, the peak period for the traps, they accounted for over 50 percent. The proportion of the catch from traps remained quite stable throughout the 1930's. A sharp decline began in the late 1940's and in 1959 the last traps were outlawed.

Regulations as to the spacing of gear worked to improve the relative productivity of the traps since the judicious location of traps on headlands and at the mouths of coves, bays, etc. prevented the use of large bodies of water by various types of mobile gear. Federal landownership meant that trap sites could not be owned outright (in fee simple) as could ordinary property. In fact, the circumstances surrounding use and transfer of these sites were peculiar, to say the least.[18] Over time "user" rights developed (without any legal sanction) to the point where sites could be bought and sold, the selling price being a measure of the capitalized rental of that particular trap site. These rights rested on continuity of use, and gradually they became the "property" of the canners—especially the large canners. The trap and its control constituted a key factor in the oligopolistic structure of the canning firms in the product market and the much greater concentration in the markets for raw fish. The trap's potential for holding live fish in inventory, also made it a bargaining instrument against the fishermen and, on occasion, a lever for short-run local buying price manipulation.

At the time of the passage of the White Act in 1924, entry conditions in the canning industry could be summarized as fol-

[18] Cooley, *op. cit.*, pp. 31 ff.

lows: the red salmon fishery in western Alaska, primarily Bristol Bay, was the most valuable segment of the fishery. It was also one of the most isolated fishing and fish processing industries in the world. Business operations could only be sustained by firms with sufficient financial strength to cope with the high overhead costs and risks associated with operating in that environment. Furthermore, there was a limited number of "good" canning sites in Bristol Bay, and the early pre-emption of these by the large packers created additional cost problems for smaller firms.[19] Hence, entry was moderately difficult.

In central and southeastern Alaska individual sites for canning plants were, on the average, less valuable, and there was considerable mitigation of the extreme conditions found to the west. In general, fishing seasons were longer and transportation more readily available. The same was true of supplies of local labor, building materials, and other operating services. Buyer concentration was lower in these areas than in Bristol Bay, but this was offset in part by the control over fish supplies conferred by control of trap sites. As indicated above, this tended to be localized, but in the aggregate it added greatly to the market power of the larger canners in acquiring fish. In the rest of Alaska, therefore, geographical and other associated barriers to entry were lower than in the western region, but the small independent entrant was faced with a fishery of lower unit value and a supply problem associated with the location and efficiency of traps in particular areas.

The preceding description of the structural development of the fishery is quite consistent with the standard hypotheses suggested by the theory of industrial organization. In its earliest stages the industry was plagued by severe price competition. This was in part a function of the open access nature of the resource and the highly elastic supply function facing new entrants. There were no substantial barriers—financial, technological, or geographic— to entry. The combination of these circumstances produced

[19] Homer E. Gregory and Kathleen Barnes, *North Pacific Fisheries*. Studies of the Pacific, No. 3 (San Francisco: American Institute of Pacific Relations, 1939), p. 120.

80

initially an unstable, atomistic industry, with frequent entry and high mortality among smaller firms.

This situation was short-lived, however. As indicated above, the combination of overexpansion and national depression provided the necessary incentive for an initially successful consolidation, and the industry was transformed into a highly concentrated oligopoly. The high degree of concentration was sustained for almost two decades in the face of several minor changes in the fishery.[20] The first was a rapid shift in supply conditions. Supplies of red salmon in central Alaska (primarily the Karluk area) and southeastern Alaska were inadequate for economic operations, and the fishery for reds was heavily concentrated on Bristol Bay. As indicated, barriers to entry were much higher in that location, which helped sustain the degree of concentration. Limited technological changes also took place. Shortly after the turn of the century, the industry shifted from essentially handicraft methods to mechanized assembly line canning techniques.[21] The improvement in techniques raised the cost of entry in the short run, but did not change the basic technological structure of the processing industry. Even with mechanization there were no substantial economies of scale in the processing of salmon beyond those achieved in a single efficient "line."

After 1909, expansion of the market led to the utilization of other species of salmon and a sharp drop in concentration. By 1920 the share of the first eight firms was down to 49 percent of the pack, and the dominant position of the first firm was greatly reduced. Entry had taken place, some of it through backward integration by large national firms, such as Libby, McNeil and Libby and—during the next decade—Nakat Packing (A&P).

[20] We consider concentration of over 70 percent of output in the hands of the first eight firms as "high" concentration. In 1909 the first eight firms accounted for 80 percent of the Alaska pack.

[21] The key change was the introduction in 1903 of a machine that could head, split, and clean the fish—the "Iron Chink." High-speed canning lines became general after World War I. See Millard C. Marsh and John N. Cobb, *The Fisheries of Alaska in 1908*, Bureau of Fisheries Document No. 645 (Washington: U.S. Government Printing Office, 1909), pp. 516–18, for a description of canning using handicraft methods.

Marketing techniques in the industry contributed to somewhat higher concentration in the product market, as many independent producers sold all or a portion of their pack to large distributors. The brokers and dealers in salmon also tended to shift a larger portion of the pack they handled toward national distributors.[22]

The widespread use of traps and the barriers associated with the geography of the fishery tended to restrict entry. On the other hand, the open access status of the resource, and the absence of any economies of scale or financial barriers to new entry suggested that these obstacles would not be proof against new competition over longer periods. The steady decline in the dominant position of the large firms after 1910 is consistent with this view.

The following hypothesis about behavior patterns follows from this profile of the industry as an oligopoly and oligopsony of moderate concentration with no strong barriers to entry. If collusion were effective in controlling both prices and entry, it could be expected that prices paid to fishermen would be relatively stable and low enough to enable the canners to show more than competitive profit rates over time. In effect, monopsony or perfectly collusive oligopsony would be tantamount to ownership of the resource and the packers would extract as much of the potential economic rent as the inherent instability of physical supply permitted. If, however, collusion were not adequate to insure joint maximization and to bar entry, a variety of undesirable results would ensue: inefficient production; a tendency toward periodic excess capacity with painful periods of readjustment; and periodically unstable prices and profits.[23]

These results are readily observed in the Alaskan salmon fishery. In equilibrium, with easy entry, the decline in concentration could be ascribed to a persistent discrepancy between price and

[22] Daniel B. DeLoach, *Salmon Canning Industry*. Oregon State Monographs, Economic Study No. 1 (Corvallis: Oregon State University, February 1939), pp. 67 ff.

[23] Profits would be unstable even under monopoly or monopsony, in view of: (1) the substantial cross-elasticity of demand between canned salmon and a wide range of other fish and canned meat products; and (2) the lag in adjustment of raw fish prices to changes in the product market. In effect, costs of each season's pack are sunk before much of it is produced.

minimum average cost. But in this instance the change in the ratio is the result of a disequilibrium situation, a secular but erratic movement of the demand function to the right. With a fixed unit of production—each season's pack—each year, rising prices tended to yield excess profits, followed by new entry. Given the high degree of uncertainty with respect to both catch and market price, profits varied widely from year to year. The variability in the price-cost ratio was aggravated by the subsidization of the entry of small companies by the manufacturers of cans.[24] On occasion, the small producer was able to obtain cans on credit, use rented machinery, and gain additional working capital from distributors in return for the privilege of marketing his pack. These various sources of funds minimized the financial barriers to entry and increased instability in the industry. Speculative entry, to make one season's pack, was easy, and its prevalence is attested by the high rate of failure among small canners.[25]

The open access status of the resources added further to the basic instability in organization. With the natural limitation on the numbers of good trap sites (and, subsequently, legal limitation on traps), geographic expansion and the exploitation of the cheaper species tended to open up new sources of supply for new entrants.

The interrelations of these structural characteristics are clearly illustrated by the problems of poaching and of trap robbing. Traps, especially those in isolated locations, were usually manned by one man. In 1919 the robbing of traps became so frequent that the industry appealed for help, and the Navy dispatched a gunboat and subchaser to Alaska.[26] Some of the larger concerns also increased the number of guards at the trap sites. In spite of these precautions, piracy (the stealing of fish held within traps) continued along with "regular" poaching (fishing in illegal areas and at illegal times). If piracy and poaching were difficult to stop at the source, they were certainly not very difficult to stop at the cannery. Both could have been largely eliminated if the canners

[24] Gregory and Barnes, *op. cit.*, p. 124.
[25] Marsh and Cobb, *op. cit.*, pp. 440 ff. Also Gregory and Barnes, *op. cit.*, p. 91.
[26] Cooley, *op. cit.*, p. 156.

had refused to buy fish believed to have come from illegal sources. During periods of expansion, however, the competition for fish was usually so severe that no questions were asked. The canneries outfitted and financed much of the redundant gear and provided a ready market for its output. Reports involving the theft and subsequent sale to canneries of fish caught in the canners' own traps were legion. Throughout the entire history of the fishery, at least until quite recently, poaching has provided a significant share, at times more than 10 percent, of the total catch.[27]

By the early 1920's the Alaskan salmon fishery had matured into a moderately concentrated oligopoly with a substantial competitive fringe. The degree of concentration varied with the geography of the fishery, and was much greater in the markets for raw fish than for end products. The industry contained firms that were subsidiaries of large national corporations, other relatively large firms that were completely integrated within the fish business, and a large number of smaller independent concerns, some partially integrated and others operating solely in one phase of the industry. Although most firms had some direct financial connection with at least a few fishermen, the open access nature of the resource plus other factors making for ease of entry meant that effective control of supply in any of the several markets for raw fish was impossible. In addition, the bargaining position of the canner *vis-à-vis* the fisherman did not encourage full integration into fishing by the canners, except in such remote areas as Bristol Bay.

The effects of the industrial instability, with its periodic bursts of new entry and failures, sharp fluctuations in prices and profits, and bitter efforts by each cannery to increase its share of fish, runs through all phases of the industry's performance. Economic instability obviously accentuated the difficulties of biological management of the fishery, both in a technical sense and in terms of cooperation between the industry and the regulatory authority. On the economic side it resulted, in the 1890's, early 1920's and

[27] In its annual review of the Alaskan fisheries, the federal government used to publish a list of violators caught and convicted in Alaska. In 1929, for example, 12 traps and 15 vessels were seized for illegal fishing in southeast Alaska alone.

1930's, and again after World War II, in periodic overcapacity in both fishing and processing facilities. The instability in the economic structure in earlier years would probably have been even greater but for the political strength of the packers.[28]

At the level of industry behavior, two characteristics stand out through the entire development period. The first was the continuing confusion noted earlier over the meaning of the conservation issue; the second, the political influence of the industry.

As we have argued above, the lack of support for (or active opposition to) effective conservation measures was not so much a result of greed as of instability in structure, the observed increase in the aggregate catch, and the general ignorance of the underlying biological parameters on the part of both the fishing industry and the "conservationists." A successful collusive oligopoly with tight control over participants and the ability to exclude new entrants should have realized the advantage of operating under a long-run concept of economic maximization. In those circumstances the industry would have responded rationally to the threat to its own welfare inherent in any deterioration in the productivity of the salmon stocks by limiting fishing effort.

However, the political pressure exerted by the industry on the old Bureau of Fisheries and its successor organizations was essentially oriented toward short-run maximization.[29] The most extensive political efforts were exercised to prevent territorial control over the fisheries, primarily to keep the traps in operation and to maintain control over fish supply. In addition to pressures at the legislative level, the industry was constantly on the Bureau's doorstep to argue for revision of regulations on an *ad hoc* basis.

The arguments for these temporary revisions were always com-

[28] The large packers were able virtually to close down the Bristol Bay fishery in 1935. The reason given was that the runs in the Bay in years divisible by five were traditionally small, which is correct. Most contemporary observers suggest, however, that the real reason was the low price of canned red salmon. The small pack of that year was followed by a sharp rise in price. The 1935 closure is also cited as an instance of the political influence of the packers with the Bureau of Fisheries in gaining legal sanction for the closure. The closure also had important employment effects which caused considerable resentment.

[29] See especially Cooley's exposition of these pressures. Cooley, *op. cit.*, Part II.

plex. First, there were serious inherent problems of management. Regulations were issued in Washington prior to the fishing season. They covered all activities in the field, and prescribed the hours of closure, length of fishing seasons, and locations where fishing was permissible. Yet the characteristics of salmon and the changing nature of the biological environment inevitably produce variations in the size, timing, and geographical distribution of runs far beyond the capacity of the regulatory agency (then or now) to predict in advance. Granted the need for generalized overall regulations that cover a wide range of variable local conditions, there was equally urgent need for short-term flexibility in application. At best, the fishermen and canners were uneasy in this procrustean bed, and at worst there was continuing resentment and even open rebellion in the face of rigid and, in many cases, ineffective rules.

This problem was never satisfactorily solved by the federal government, and it was not until the reorganization of Alaskan regulations in the 1950's that significant progress toward a solution was made. The great need was for flexible regulations that could be adjusted in the field to meet local conditions: to open seasons early when runs came early; to close them when only small runs appeared; to extend seasons when needed to catch fish in excess of needed escapement; to permit fishing in certain areas and not in others. In the period prior to the early 1920's, the government did not have the biological knowledge of the runs needed to make a detailed management program meaningful. Flexible regulations might have eliminated some of the antagonism to management (and perhaps also some of the charges of favoritism), even when used on the basis of extremely fragmentary knowledge of the essential relations among catch, escapement, and the number of returnees in the subsequent cycle years.

The size of the pack was initially limited by the canners' collective *ex ante* estimate of market demand. Each concern took the required number of cans north each year, and when these were filled the season was over. Pressure to extend seasons gradually developed as biological constraints reduced the prospective elasticity of supply in the face of secular increases in demand. If, for any number of reasons, such as bad weather or the late arrival of the fish, it was expected that "the pack would not have been made" at the closing date,[30] the industry frequently put pressure on the administrators of the regulations to eliminate weekly closures, extend seasons, or permit fishing in more advantageous locations. These pressures were due in large part to the structure of the processing sector. A single-firm monopoly (or monopsony) exploiting the fishery would have had both incentive and means to maximize over a longer time horizon; and, as a corollary, to press for and support research leading to more meaningful and flexible regulations. The existing firms could only struggle for their share of the supply, and, in years of shortage, press for more fish, regardless of the biological consequences. They were frequently successful in persuading the government, often over the advice of the biologists in the field, to modify regulations in the desired direction.

It is not surprising that the canners' lobby was as powerful as it was. It spoke for a well-defined set of business interests in the state of Washington and, to a lesser extent, in California and Oregon. Fishing is an important industry in those states, especially in Washington, and the political influence of the processing firms in the west coast states was high. In general, the political positions adopted by the processors were supported by the unions and also by other interests such as the Alaskan Steamship Company.

The fishery itself was isolated geographically from the general check of public opinion and also by public ignorance of the technical nature of fishery management. The Territory had no effective lobby or political organization. Since congressional delegations seldom visited Alaska, opinion within the Territory was not widely understood in Washington, and even when it was, it had no power position in the Congress with which to oppose the activities of the canners. Moreover, the Territorial "position" was rarely, if ever, based on analysis any more firmly rooted in fact than that of the canners. The struggles occurred over the shares of the income, profits, and employment at stake, and hence over the types of fishing gear to be used and by whom. To the

[30] That is, if the bulk of the plants had not utilized fully the "lump" of capacity planned at the beginning of the season.

rest of the nation, fishery matters were relatively unimportant, and although occasional administrators or members of Congress realized the situation created by the dominant position of the industry, no outside champion could effectively redress the balance of power.

The crucial element in the contest between the politically powerful and articulate canners' lobby, the proponents of more vigorous and "scientific" salmon management, and the pleaders for Alaskan local interests was the inadequacy of the biological data. As long as the gross catch continued to rise, and indeed as long as depletion did not become painfully apparent to all, it was relatively easy to persuade Washington that "since the runs were later this year, it is in the best interest of all, including conservationists, to extend the season for 48 hours." The biological argument had to be developed in its full complexity before the necessity of particular conservation practices could be justified. When no one could say with reasonable certainty what really had to be done to conserve the fish, it was very difficult for the administrators not to go along with industry requests. In these circumstances, the pressure from processors to increase and extend fishing effort was greatest in poor years when the runs were most vulnerable, a situation which further aggravated the biological problem.[31] Therefore the industry, which appeared to Alaskans to be a monopolized economic structure, did not control the fishery in the one crucial sense in which purely private monopolistic control would really have operated, at least partially, in the public interest. And, in all honesty, it appears in retrospect that the basic political conflict was not entirely between the canners and the proponents of sound management, but also between the canners and local residents over division of the spoils.

[31] Gilbert and O'Malley, *op. cit.*, p. 150.

CHAPTER 6

History of Regulation in Alaska

The biological and economic effects of regulation prior to 1924 have been analyzed in considerable detail elsewhere.[1] Therefore it is necessary at this point only to review the history of regulation from its inception until 1924 to establish the position of the control agencies relative to the fishery and to summarize the effects of the White Act on the industry.

COMMERCIAL FISHERY REGULATIONS PRIOR TO THE WHITE ACT

Regulation in the Alaska salmon fishery has dealt with one or more of the following variables: types of gear, fishing time (the specification of periods of time when it is legal to fish), fishing areas, licenses and taxes, and the operation of hatcheries. Since the mid-1950's, combined regulation of gear, time, and area has been attempted through a program that requires pre-season registration of the gear to be fished in a given area. Once a unit of gear is registered in a particular area, it is restricted to fishing

[1] See especially Richard A. Cooley, *Politics and Conservation: The Decline of the Alaska Salmon* (New York: Harper & Row, 1963), Part II.

in that area in that year. By 1903 practically all types of regulations had been applied to the Alaskan fishery.[2]

In the initial stages, the legislation and regulations affecting Alaska salmon were indicative of congressional intent rather than operational programs. The Act of 1889 prohibited the use of barricades and called for investigations of the fisheries. But no money was appropriated to implement the Act until 1892 when funds were provided for one inspector and an assistant.

The next important legislation was the Act of 1896. It contained, among other provisions, the first modest step toward termination of fishing activities in the mouths of streams (where even mobile gear is quite capable of exterminating individual runs) by prohibiting fishing above tidewater in streams less than 500 feet in width. The subsequent history of regulations on this point has been an extension of this basic position, forcing the fishermen away from the fresh water out into the bays and estuaries. The fish have a tendency to "school up" while waiting to ascend into fresh water, and these regulations are aimed at preventing the capture of entire schools when the fish are especially vulnerable.

The biological effects of this type of regulation are mixed, however. The analogy that best describes this process is to compare the transition from the salt to fresh water to a funneling process. Clearly, fishing effort is more efficient if applied in the area of greatest fish density, the neck of the funnel; and in any program that considers economic rationalization of the fishery, the efficiency criterion is of great importance.

Two objections stand in the way of its full implementation. The first is institutional and, to a certain extent, legal. Management on this basis would involve complete reorganization of the fishery and economic regulation at a level of sophistication beyond that implicit in the mere erection of barriers to entry.

The second difficulty is biological. If fishing occurs in the

---

[2] An enumeration of the laws and regulations from 1889 to the White Act (1924) is given in Willis H. Rich and Edward M. Ball, *Statistical Review of Alaska Salmon Fisheries.* Bureau of Fisheries Document No. 1041 (Washington: U.S. Government Printing Office, 1928), p. 60. See also Cooley, *op. cit.,* chapters 4 and 5.

stream or at its mouth, the full burden of the fishing effort may
fall on a particular race of fish. If, however, the effort is transferred to more open water where the races of fish tend to be
mixed, a more random distribution of effort on various stocks is
obtained. In the absence of explicit knowledge of the timing and
migration paths of each group and accurate control over escapement of each, this would provide, up to a point, a more desirable
biological pattern of escapement than would indiscriminate
harvesting of salmon at points where particular sub-groups are
fully separated. On the other hand, harvesting of mixed stocks
involves the inherent danger that those of less productivity will
be overexploited when exposed to a common rate of fishing.
Eventually, of course, the additional cost of pushing the fishery
further out to sea would overtake the incremental gains. The
proper demarcation of this point would depend on a host of
factors specific to each fishery area, and would require a degree
of knowledge of the populations involved and a sampling program far beyond our present or prospective capabilities.

In brief, the tendency to push the fishery farther from the
stream mouth has steadily decreased efficiency in the fishery.[3] At
the same time, it probably has provided some biological and
economic benefits by reducing the pressure on particular races of
fish and providing more uniform quality of fish taken. The
opinions of biologists are mixed on this point. It is impossible to
specify the magnitude of the benefits that have occurred, but
there is enough agreement to suggest that the benefits are real,
given the inability to control the number of fishing units or the
biological knowledge to identify and manage individual races
with precision. In Bristol Bay, where such knowledge does exist,
it is clearly desirable, on both biological and economic grounds,
to place the fishery at the mouths of the five major stream-lake
systems.

A further major step in the regulatory program was taken in
1900. The Act of 1896 was modified and extended and the canneries were required to establish hatcheries. This hatchery pro-

[3] Elimination of the traps, however, resulted in much greater purse seine
catches in areas closer to stream mouths, particularly in the central and
southeast Alaska pink fishery.

gram (which only applied to red salmon) was a failure. However, the potential contribution of hatcheries to maintenance or enhancement of salmon catches for other species remains an unsettled issue, even today. It seems unlikely that any general basis for assessing the success of a hatchery program will be developed in the near future. To the casual observer, on a purely *a priori* basis, the hatchery appears to be a "put and take" operation, very similar to stocking a heavily fished trout stream prior to the opening of the season. This oversimplified view of the role of the hatchery has played an important part in the regulatory history of the fishery, with the effect, intentional or not, of delaying more stringent controls. If it were correct, regulation of the salmon fishery would be made much easier, but the essential economic irrationality of unrestricted entry would still preclude any long-run increase in the net yield of the fishery. If the supply of fish could be maintained or expanded by the hatcheries, the resulting maintenance or expansion of excess capacity would still dissipate all or most of the potential net yield generated by initial incremental catch value in excess of hatchery costs.

The fervent belief in hatcheries as the long-run solution to overfishing carried great weight for a prolonged period, especially from the time of the enactment of the hatchery requirement (1900) to World War I. The idea that the stock could be maintained at some optimal level by artificial means encouraged disregard for regulation and invited even more careless exploitation of the resources.

Thus far only chinook and coho salmon have been reared in hatcheries with any degree of success (measured in terms of contributions to the commercial catch). Scientific rearing of salmon in significant quantities presents genetic and technical problems that *today* rule out any general or complete substitution of hatchery production for natural reproduction. The entire subject remains a major research problem for both federal and state fishery agencies, particularly when the option is complete abandonment of a run. In recent years the hatchery picture, at least for chinooks and cohoes, has brightened enough to encourage benefit-cost analysis of the operations by the Department of Fisheries of the state of Washington. The results to date are encouraging in enough cases to warrant further effort, and the results of a major program to assess the contribution of the Columbia River hatcheries will be of great interest.

The final major regulatory technique—limitation of fishing time—was introduced in the Acts of 1896 and 1903. The former set weekly closures in certain areas, and the latter (repealed in the following year) made June 30 the opening day of the season in southeast Alaska. Over the years, adjustment of fishing time has developed into the principal regulatory instrument. In some cases—Bristol Bay, for example—regulation of fishing time has gone so far as to prescribe the hours of the day that are open. And, as indicated above, time closures, together with area restriction on gear, became, in the 1950's, the first tentative step toward regulation for economic objectives.

The biological effects of time closures are far more complex than they appear at first glance. If the fishery could be represented as a continuous and constant flow of fish through time, the selection for escapement and exposure to the commercial fishery of various segments of the flow on essentially a random basis would have very little impact on the biological characteristics of the run. These assumptions are not met, however; the flow of fish is erratic, both in the aggregate and for particular races. The flow of individual runs is generally severely peaked. In Bristol Bay, for example, the bulk of the fish in the entire complex of runs may come and go in less than 15 days. From year to year and within each year there are significant variations in timing and amplitude of the returning run of each race of fish. In some streams, spawners ascend at a steady pace, while in others they appear in dispersed clusters with no apparent pattern. Local conditions, such as water temperature, turbidity, and the rate of stream flow, materially influence the movement of the fish.

In the face of these variables, the sampling process imposed on the fishery by the timing of the closures ceases to be even approximately random. A weekend closing may permit an entire run to escape; conversely, a midweek opening may permit heavy inroads on any particular race. Similarly, opening and closing dates for the season have important population effects. Very early and very late runs may escape the fishery. If they do, these fish may benefit further from the impact of predation on those runs that are subject to the fishery.

Other effects involve long-term changes as a result of the pattern of removal and the shifts in the timing of the runs. For example, if the survivors of any run tend to be those which arrive last, after the peak of the run has occurred, the peak of the run may gradually shift to a later date. These conditions are interrelated with the process of extension of the fishery in time and space. Except in a few specific cases (e.g., the fishing at Karluk) little quantitative knowledge exists as to the shifts that have occurred for the whole complex of Pacific salmon runs. Nevertheless, biologists are in general agreement that this technique of regulation has influenced the timing of many runs, and, in some instances, the biological characteristics of the stocks exploited.

The last major congressional regulatory act prior to the White Act was passed in 1906. It extended the provisions of previous acts and also introduced license fees and taxes. The taxes on canned salmon were tied to the hatchery provisions by a rebate plan.

From 1906 to 1924 many additional regulations were promulgated by the governing agency,[4] which extended and refined the basic regulatory instruments and procedures described above. This process was continuous, and by 1924 there was an extensive body of regulations covering most aspects of the fishery. Economic criteria for regulation of the fishery were not included in these rules, but the need for some economic controls had been suggested twice: in 1906 by David Starr Jordan and Barton W. Evermann; and in 1919, more explicitly, by Gilbert and O'Malley.[5]

[4] In 1903 the Bureau of Fisheries was created in the Department of Commerce and Labor. This superseded the older U.S. Fisheries Commission in the Treasury Department, and was itself superseded by the Bureau of Commercial Fisheries in the Department of the Interior.

[5] David S. Jordan and Barton W. Evermann, Preliminary Report of the Alaska Salmon Commission. House Document 477, 56th Congress, 2nd Session (Washington: U.S. Government Printing Office, 1906). C. H. Gilbert and Henry O'Malley, "Special Investigations of the Salmon Fishery in Central and Western Alaska," Alaska Fishery and Fur-Seal Industries in 1919, Bureau of Fisheries (Washington: U.S. Government Printing Office, 1920).

Unfortunately, as noted above, a great gap existed between *de jure* regulations and *de facto* practices. For example, in 1908, Marsh and Cobb reported as follows:[6]

In view of reports early in the season that the trap-net fishermen were not going to observe the law, the waters of southeast Alaska were very thoroughly patrolled this year, and a cruise by the assistant agent in Stephens Passage, Lynn Canal, Chatham and Icy Straits, extending from Saturday, July 4, to Monday afternoon, July 6, covering some 300 miles and including visits to 38 traps, complete and in process of construction, disclosed a most remarkable condition of affairs. Of the 34 traps operating, 29 were brazenly violating the law, 4 were guilty of minor or technical violations and but one trap was confining strictly to the letter of the law.

Violation of regulations was endemic in the fishery, and regardless of the merits of regulation, enforcement was virtually impossible. From 1892 to 1910 one man and an assistant were responsible for all Alaskan enforcement. By 1913 there were four men assigned to the task. And from 1906 to 1915 less than $5 thousand was spent on research.

THE WHITE ACT

In the broadest sense, the White Act was the product of three forces: the biological state of the salmon resource; the economic condition of the Alaska fishing industry; and political attitudes in Washington, D.C.

In the summer of 1919, C. H. Gilbert and Henry O'Malley carried out an investigation of the fishery. Their report summarized and stated forcefully the feelings of some biologists concerned with the Alaska salmon stocks. They charged that the evidence pointing to overfishing was clear, and suggested that the necessity for economic regulation was self-evident in the rapid increase in inputs of men and equipment with no corresponding increase in the yield. This perceptive report indicated a partial understanding of the necessity of formulating a regulatory program consistent with both biological constraints on out-

[6] Millard C. Marsh and John N. Cobb, *The Fisheries of Alaska in 1908*, Bureau of Fisheries Document No. 645 (Washington: U.S. Government Printing Office, 1909).

put and the price-profit motivated reactions of fishermen and processors. While biologists were by no means unanimous in their evaluation of the state of the salmon stocks or of the measures required to protect them, there was general concern for the future.

The industry had expanded rapidly during World War I. In 1915 there were some 86 canneries operating in Alaska, and by 1920 this number had jumped to 143. Almost 6.7 million cases were packed in 1918. After the war, in 1919, the government cancelled its contracts and returned its unused supplies to the packers. These heavy inventories presented difficult financial problems for the overexpanded industry, and prices broke sharply as dumping developed. In 1919 the opening price for red salmon (per dozen one-pound cans) was $3.35, up $1.00 from 1918. In 1920 the market opened at $3.25, down 10 cents, and by 1921 it had fallen to $2.35.[7] The general economic depression which began in January 1920 complicated the problems of the industry, and a number of failures occurred among the canning firms. These economic pressures altered industry attitudes sharply, and conservation suddenly became good business as well as good biology.[8] This position relaxed somewhat as prices stabilized in 1922 and 1923, but at least part of the impetus for legislation reflected the weak economic position of the industry.

Finally, Secretary of Commerce Hoover was favorably disposed toward the conservation issue and was prepared to accept the increase in the regulatory powers of his Department required to mount a more effective program.

The legislation that emerged in 1924 was a compromise between economic interests and biological necessity. With two major exceptions the Act represented an extension of the existing pattern of regulation. The first change, in Section 6, involved the scope of federal authority and penalties for the violation of regulations. As had been suggested by Gilbert and O'Malley, this change put the regulatory process more on a par with that in continental United States by giving the Bureau the legal power to arrest and also to seize gear. The latter was a more serious

[7] *Pacific Fisherman Yearbook*, 1918–22.
[8] For a detailed account of these attitudes see Cooley, *op. cit.*, pp. 109 ff.

threat to fishermen and canners than the usual small fines, and its implementation caused widespread resentment against the Bureau.

The most striking innovation, however, was in Section 2 of the Act, which required not less than 50 percent escapement in most streams. This meant that the commercial fishery had to be regulated in such a manner as to allow 50 percent of the fish in any given stream to escape the fishery. Unfortunately, the application of a rigid percentage escapement rule, like almost all other inflexible regulations, is not well adapted to the peculiar characteristics of the Pacific salmon. Depending on the size of the returning run, a 50 percent harvest could easily be either too large or too small for optimal escapement.

More interesting are the implications of the rule for the regulatory agency. A policy aimed at maintenance of maximum sustained yield through assurance of adequate escapement requires the regulatory agency to mount a research and enforcement effort sufficient for the task. At the time the White Act was passed only a few persons had any real grasp of the complexity of the regulatory problem. The development of an organization capable of carrying out the requirements of the Act would have taken many years in the best of circumstances. In the face of subsequent congressional neglect, partisan sniping, and conflicting pressures from vested interests, only very modest results could have been expected. The lack of general recognition of the difficulties became a source of disappointment and disillusionment with the results achieved under the Act.

At first, however, the industry thought highly of the Act, and this opinion was reflected in the trade journals. Some 15 years later, Gregory and Barnes, without adequate knowledge of the biological situation, could regard the Act as

...making possible greater production of salmon than previously, yet this has taken place despite the restrictions imposed to insure proper escapement, and therefore presumably without jeopardizing the future.[9]

[9] Homer E. Gregory and Kathleen Barnes, *North Pacific Fisheries*, Studies of the Pacific, No. 3 (San Francisco: American Institute of Pacific Relations, 1939).

Writing in the late 1930's, they could not foresee the catastrophic decline in the fishery that was to come, nor could they appreciate the inadequacy of both the research and enforcement capabilities of the regulatory agency.

Other authors were critical of the Act for other reasons. Writing in the 1950's, Ernest Gruening emphasized what eventually was recognized as a key omission in the Act from the standpoint of the emerging regional consciousness of the Territorial residents:

> By the White Act of 1924, Congress had foreclosed Alaskans' principal aspiration—control of their fisheries.[10]

By any reasonable standards the program developed under the Act of 1924 must, in retrospect, be judged a failure. Certainly it did not prevent depletion of the fishery. Yet, once the self-delusion about the status of the resource had been dispelled in the 1950's, the Act became the basis of a greatly expanded federal program of research and enforcement. In spite of the provision about escapement and the penalties provided for enforcement, however, the Act really did not change *de facto* conditions in the fishery. The status quo was maintained after 1924 largely as before.

BOOM AND BUST: 1924 TO STATEHOOD

After the contraction in the fishery in the early 1920's, the industry began to expand again in the latter part of the decade. New firms entered and some mergers occurred. The most important entrant was Nakat Packing (A&P) and the key merger, the creation of the Alaskan Pacific Salmon Company in 1928. After 1924, prices rose sharply, fluctuated around those higher levels until 1928, then began to decline again. The entries and mergers that took place, in part as a result of financial speculation, did not change the basic structure of the industry.

There were other changes, perhaps the most significant being the introduction of high-speed canning lines in 1926 and exten-

[10] Ernest Gruening, *The State of Alaska* (New York: Random House, 1954), p. 282.

sion of the market by vigorous national advertising. The level of industry activity continued to respond to market conditions, with heavy pressure to pack as much as possible as long as price expectations were firm, and to curtail operations (as in Bristol Bay in 1935) when they were not. Prices showed severe cyclical variations. The opening price for reds (per dozen one-pound cans) dropped from $3.10 in 1930 to $1.45 in 1932. Thereafter it recovered, and the industry began another period of expansion.

During the initial stages of the depression, economy measures in the federal government curtailed the already slender enforcement capability in Alaska. The aerial survey program was cut back and the number of stream guards reduced. There was some increase in enforcement later in the decade but expenditures for research were minimal, averaging less than $25,000 per year until 1939.

With the outbreak of war in 1939, price increases put more and more pressure on the resource. The price of salmon rose 63 percent from 1940 to 1942—an increase of 25 percent even after adjustment for changes in the general price level. At this point, the catch began to decline, a development that simply intensified the industry's efforts to obtain relaxation of regulations.

During the 1930's a more cohesive and vocal Alaskan position toward regulation was developing.[11] This position gradually polarized around two central issues: opposition to outside interests and dissatisfaction with federal control. Public concern with both matters increased in the later 1930's and came to a head in 1939. Early in that year the Commissioner of Fisheries resigned. In May the Bureau of Fisheries was transferred to the Department of the Interior and became part of the Fish and Wildlife Service, and in July the House of Representatives passed a resolution calling for a congressional investigation of the administration of the Alaska fishery. The principal result of the investigation was to break down some of the isolation surrounding the industry. For the first time Congressmen were exposed to a full airing of the divergent interests in the Alaska fisheries: the complaints of Alaskans, mostly directed against traps and absen-

[11] George W. Rogers, *The Future of Alaska* (Baltimore: The Johns Hopkins Press, 1962), chapter 5.

99

tee administration; the attitudes of the canners; and the actual operating conditions in Alaska. Despite evidence of congressional dissatisfaction (and confusion) over the situation, the advent of war in 1941 prevented any major overhauling of administrative programs.

As indicated in the discussion of the Bristol Bay fishery, there was a strong tendency to rationalize the economic structure of the fishery during World War II. Regulations were relaxed, the fishery moved further inshore, fishing was permitted in areas previously restricted, and canners were required to consolidate operations in a limited number of joint units. For example, in 1942 the Bristol Bay season was allowed to open two weeks earlier than usual and the midweek closing was suspended, and in 1943 only 83 canneries operated in all of Alaska. Military security requirements and the drain on manpower in the fishery reduced the number and range of operating units to a point where relatively full and efficient utilization of gear became possible.

The trend of output continued downward, however. Landings of salmon averaged 560 million pounds during the 1935–39 period. During the war (1940–44), despite curtailment of the number of operating units, the catch had dropped to 453 million pounds, and in the immediate postwar period (1945–49) it was only 381 million pounds—a 32 percent decline over the decade. In the 1950's, the catch declined further to a 259 million pound yearly average for the next five years, and only moderate recovery in the 1960's seems indicated. These aggregate figures conceal much greater variation in the catch by species and in the finer detail of yield by species, by area, or by particular race of fish.

This was the pattern predicted in 1919, when Gilbert and O'Malley had written (in reference to the Kvichak-Naknek area in Bristol Bay):

The sequence of events is always the same. Decreased production is accomplished by increase of gear. Fluctuations in the seasons become more pronounced. Good seasons still appear in which nearly maximum packs are made. But the poor seasons become more numerous. When poor seasons appear no attempt is made to compensate by fishing less closely. On the contrary, efforts are redoubled to put up the full pack.

100

The poorer years strike constantly lower levels, until it is apparent to all that serious depletion has occurred.[12]

This behavior hypothesis was supported by the investigations of Rich and Ball and was consistent with the general decline in the fishery.[13]

In addition to the decline in abundance, the postwar period produced a shift in the political situation in Alaska. In 1940 Ernest Gruening was elected Governor. One of his proposals involved a basic tax reform program that was bitterly opposed by the Alaska fishing and mining industries. The ultimate passage of this program in 1949 marked, in the opinion of one observer, the end of effective opposition by the salmon lobby in the Territory.[14] In 1949 the Territorial legislature also established a Department of Fisheries. This was a shadow department, assisting and supplementing by means of Territorial appropriations the work of the U.S. Bureau of Commercial Fisheries. It also provided the training ground necessary for eventual assumption of control by the state.

As indicated above, production fell sharply in the 1950's to the level of output prevailing before World War I. Specific areas were very hard hit and political pressures increased further. In a statewide referendum in 1952 Alaskans voted 20,500 to 5,500 to request Congress to turn control of the fisheries over to the Territory on the grounds that local management would be better management.[15] The publication of Gruening's book in 1954 restated the Territorial version of the history of congressional neglect, the power of the lobbies, and the case for statehood. From that time, given the level of economic development reached in Alaska and the hardening of political attitudes, it seems probable that a shift to state control was inevitable, especially since no rehabilitation program for the fishery, no matter how well conceived, could be effective in the short run.

There were two other structural changes of great importance in the overall salmon management program. The decline in land-

[12] C. H. Gilbert and Henry O'Malley, *op. cit.*, p. 151.
[13] Rich and Ball, *op. cit.*, p. 65.
[14] Rogers, *op. cit.*, pp. 255 ff.
[15] Gruening, *op. cit.*, p. 406.

ings forced the government and the industry to turn to a greatly expanded program of biological research. Expenditures on research by the Bureau of Commercial Fisheries were less than $100,000 per year until 1948. By 1956 they had reached almost a quarter of a million, and in 1959, the last year before statehood, they exceeded $900,000. In addition, the industry supported the formation, in 1947, of the Fisheries Research Institute at the University of Washington, largely because of dissatisfaction with the level and orientation of the federal program. Today the Institute, in cooperation with the federal and state programs, provides for a broad-based attack on the complex biological problems of the fishery. The Institute has been supported financially by both the industry and the Bureau of Commercial Fisheries, and the latter is currently the major contributor.

Fully as important as the biological factors, and largely misunderstood or ignored in the political debate, were the massive economic problems of the fishery. In addition to the core problems of inefficiency and the stifling effect of regulation on innovation and technical progressiveness, the spectre of unemployment in the precarious Alaskan economy and the special role of the immobile native fishermen have exerted constant pressure on the fishery administrators.

The problems posed by the economics of the fishery have been as ubiquitous as the problem of depletion. Pre-World War I proposals for economic controls included suggestions that both fishing units and the number of canneries in an area be limited. After the war Gilbert and O'Malley emphatically stated the need for economic control, and during World War II, in a proposed revision of the White Act, detailed legislation was presented that included direct measures for economic regulation.[16] Finally, the problem of the amount of fishing effort and its regulation weighed heavily on the minds of those who formulated the revised federal regulatory program in the 1950's. All these efforts suffered from the same deficiency that had plagued those charged with formulation of meaningful biological regulations: the lack of detailed empirical and theoretical economic knowledge of the

[16] Hearings on S.930, Committee on Commerce, January 20, 1944. See the report of the Secretary of the Interior and amendments, pp. 97–98.

fishery, which made it impossible to specify the implications and costs of unrestricted entry.

In spite of the long history of bad feelings, the transfer of regulatory authority over the fisheries to the state was accomplished smoothly. The Alaskan department already in existence had established its competence. Its much greater public acceptance made its task easier, and thus far it has retained this respect. Operating details of the conservation problem are obviously easier to administer from Juneau than from Washington, although today there are many issues, primarily international, that are basically beyond the capacity of any state to handle in a satisfactory manner, and some critical potential conflicts between state and national interest are yet to be faced.

Within the existing framework, the question of economic performance of the industry under regulation remains the overriding issue. The furor over the Japanese high-seas fishery and the recent mild upturn in the catch have tended to obscure this question, but the state can ill afford, either in terms of its own needs or as an instrument in international bargaining, to let the fishery dissipate millions each year in manifestly inefficient operations. In the following chapter we turn to an assessment of this situation.

CHAPTER 7

Potential Economic Yield
from the Alaska Salmon Fisheries

~~~~~~

The argument of Chapters 2 through 6 has stressed the inevitability of economic waste under unrestricted salmon fishing; and, equally important, of both waste and confusion in any management program not geared, at least in part, to the objective of economic efficiency in harvesting the resource. The failure of the White Act was rooted in the inability to define the necessary and sufficient conditions for maximization of the physical yield from the resource. Similarly, the failure even to formulate meaningful economic criteria for regulation of the fishery has largely been due to the inability to define properly and to quantify the potential net economic yield. Only when it is possible to supply reasonable estimates of the amount of economic rent that is dissipated in the fishery under open access can the importance of the cost effects of regulation and the economic reaction of the fisherman to alternative controls be brought home to administrators and legislators.

Establishment of the cost of the economic waste inherent in an open access fishery regulated in terms of physical yields is the first step toward rational resource utilization. Moreover, as suggested in Chapter 2, the establishment of defensible estimates of potential net economic yield may provide at least partial protection of the salmon as a competitor for water resources in benefit-cost analysis in multiple-purpose river development programs. It is therefore crucial to make some finding as to the magnitude of the economic cost of a management program that cannot control the number of units employed (and that reduces the efficiency of individual units as a matter of policy). Are the stakes high enough to warrant a revised concept and technique of regulation?

As in most economic problems, quantification of the rent that is dissipated in the Alaska salmon fishery calls for statistical data that are not readily or directly available. For 60 years regulatory policy has concentrated on preventing improvements in technical efficiency, and it is quite impossible to estimate what the technology of the fishery would be had innovation been encouraged. Even within the framework of existing techniques, the data on historical costs and yields, required to give precision to rent estimates, are lacking. Fortunately, it has been possible, in one key instance, to construct what appears to be a meaningful index of the rents involved in the fishery. While extrapolation, here as elsewhere, is a hazardous process, the conservative nature of the yield index constructed below for the Bristol Bay fishery provides the basis for at least a minimal estimate of the rent dissipated in one important segment of the Alaska salmon fishery.

In this chapter we set out the basis for estimation of the rent dissipated in the Bristol Bay fishery. A similar estimate for the Puget Sound fishery, using different techniques, is set forth in Chapter 9, and a very rough judgment as to the potential yield for other Pacific salmon fisheries is included in Chapter 10.

THE RED SALMON FISHERY OF BRISTOL BAY

The red salmon fishery of Bristol Bay may be considered a special case within the general framework of the Alaskan salmon fishery for several reasons.[1]

(1) The fishery lies on the north side of the Alaskan peninsula. Sea transportation to the Bay must cross the Gulf of Alaska, go west along the peninsula to Unimak Pass and then return east-

[1] There is only a minor fishery for other species in the Bay.

ward to reach the Bay. It is a long trip and, for small fishing craft, a dangerous one. Therefore, this fishery is the most isolated major segment of the Alaskan salmon fishery, and transportation problems and costs play a major role in the organization and conduct of the fishery.

(2) The season is extremely short, usually less than four weeks, and the unit value of the catch is high.

(3) Because of the heavy overhead costs and the short fishing period, this segment of the fishery has been dominated by the larger packers to a greater extent than the rest of the Alaskan fishery.

(4) The technology of the fishery is simpler than elsewhere in Alaska. Basically, only one kind of gear—the drift gill net—is employed. Traps were never a problem in the Bay; a few were used early in the history of this fishery but disappeared before 1923.[2] A minor fraction of the catch is landed by set nets.

(5) In recent years the biological research program in the Bay has been the most advanced in Alaska. The sophistication of this program—a combination of state, federal, and privately financed research—is illustrated by the level of biological knowledge and the techniques employed in forecasting the runs. (As indicated in Table 3, however, there is still room for refinement and improvement.) The research program began to assume its present form only in the middle 1950's, however, and because of the four- and five-year life cycle of the red salmon, the full measure of improvement in the biological basis for regulation has yet to be realized.

(6) The Bristol Bay fishery has been affected more than any other North American salmon fishery by the Japanese high-seas salmon operation.

These conditions all apply in varying degrees to the rest of the Alaskan salmon fishery, but they are or have been most pronounced in Bristol Bay. Over the years there have been changes in the relative importance of these various factors and a reduction in the isolation of the Bristol Bay fishery. Since World War II, improved transportation, especially air travel, has made entry

[2] Willis H. Rich and Edward M. Ball, *Statistical Review of Alaska Salmon Fisheries.* Bureau of Fisheries Document No. 1041 (Washington: U.S. Government Printing Office, 1928).

Table 3. Total Bristol Bay Run and Forecast of the Run, 1960–67

(*millions of fish*)

Year	Total run[a]	Forecast
1960	42.6	35.0
1961	26.3	27.0
1962	12.3	9.7
1963	8.6	15.6
1964	13.4	17.7
1965	64.0	27.8
1966	32.7 (33.8)[b]	20.6
1967	15.7 (21.5)[b]	12.3

[a] The total run includes the spawning escapement, the inshore catch, and the Japanese high-seas catches of maturing fish in the year of the run and the immature fish in their penultimate year of life in the year preceding the run.

[b] Figures in parentheses are estimates from high-seas counts.

Sources: Runs—1960–64, Alaska Department of Fish and Game, informational leaflet No. 59; 1965, Alaska Department of Fish and Game (December 1965). Forecasts—1960, Fisheries Research Institute, Circular No. 122 (mimeo); 1961, A.D.F. & G. memorandum No. 1 (mimeo); 1962–65, A.D.F. & G. informational leaflets Nos. 14, 23, 39, and 59; 1966–67, by letter from Fisheries Research Institute.

easier and thereby affected the structure of the fishery and the independence of the fishermen in the Bay. At the same time, the decline in abundance of fish has forced consolidation of canneries, and only limited entry by smaller processors has taken place.

THE STRUCTURE OF THE FISHERY

Salmon was being packed at Bristol Bay as early as 1884.[3] By 1900 over 8.5 million fish were taken. In 1903 the fishery was considered mature when the catch reached 16.3 million fish, and in 1917 the catch was 24.5 million. This figure was not approached thereafter until the extraordinary catch in 1965, which was followed by very disappointing runs in 1966 and 1967.

From the beginning, the salmon-packing operations were dominated by the larger firms. For example, in 1937 seven firms packed 91 percent of the output in western Alaska.[4] The greater

[3] *Ibid.*, p. 53.

[4] Homer E. Gregory and Kathleen Barnes, *North Pacific Fisheries*, Studies of the Pacific, No. 3 (San Francisco: American Institute of Pacific Relations, 1939), p. 120.

concentration among the packers in the Bay is shown by comparison with all of Alaska. In 1930 the first seven firms accounted for only 49 percent of the total Alaskan pack and in 1940 the first seven had 45 percent. The higher concentration among the packers in Bristol Bay was largely a result of the remote, primitive environment and the resulting overhead costs. The canneries had to provide all the facilities for living, fishing, and processing the catch during the short season. Labor and material costs naturally were higher in the Bay and constituted an additional financial barrier to entry that was not present to the same degree in central and southeast Alaska. Finally, the number of good locations available for canneries was limited, and when these were pre-empted, entry was further restricted.

Concentration in the processing sector was reflected in labor arrangements. Prior to the 1930's, the union was actually able to exclude Alaskans, both native and white, from the fishery.[5] This exclusion broke down during the 1930's, largely because of increased political pressure within the Territory, and by the end of the decade the practice of using Alaskans was established. Until 1951, however, all gear, boats, and nets used in the Bay were owned by the companies. Since then, the combination of the declining catch, improved transportation, and more efficient regulation has given rise to the utilization of some independently owned fishing equipment.

In one respect the behavior of the industry in Bristol Bay was consistent with its behavior elsewhere in Alaska. In spite of the high degree of concentration, the industry did not behave as a rational monopolist with respect to proper time rate of use of the resource. This may have been due in part to inadequate biological knowledge and an earlier irrational belief that there was no limit to abundance. (When the runs in Alaska as a whole declined so markedly after World War II, the industry responded with contributions for a research program.) A more plausible explanation is that even with the degree of control that rested in the hands of the major Bristol Bay fisheries, the oligopolistic

[5] Richard A. Cooley, *Politics and Conservation: The Decline of the Alaska Salmon* (New York: Harper & Row, 1963), pp. 52, 53. See also Gregory and Barnes, *op. cit.*, p. 200.

structure of firms throughout the Alaskan fishery was, for reasons discussed earlier, basically unstable, and this instability influenced industry behavior in the Bay as well as elsewhere.

The outstanding physical characteristic of the Bristol Bay red salmon fishery in recent years has been the wide variation in the runs. During the 1950's, year-to-year variation in yields ran from several hundred percent above to 50 percent below mean values. Based on five-year averages, output has fallen almost continuously from the 1930's through the 1950's. The 1963–67 average catch of approximately 10 million fish contrasts sharply with the 1934–39 average of 17 million. Recently, the dramatically improved conservation programs initiated in the 1950's seem to have taken hold, and catches during the early 1960's suggest a possible reversal in the long downward trend. The evidence is not conclusive, however. The spectacularly large run in 1965 was followed by a mediocre run in 1966, and 1967 was a disaster. (See Figure 11.)

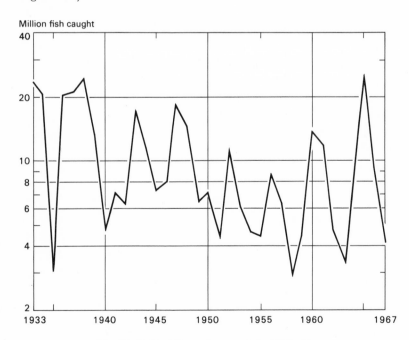

Fig. 11. Bristol Bay salmon catch, 1933–67.
Source: Table A–5.

109

The decline in abundance of reds has been accompanied by nearly proportional price increases. By the late 1950's the money value of the catch was actually 45 percent greater than in the 1930's. The real price of fish (i.e., the actual price adjusted for changes in the general level of prices) has also risen but not enough to offset the decline in physical yield. The real value of the catch was 37 percent lower in the late 1950's than in the 1930's, but was considerably higher in the 1950's than in the 1940's.

These fluctuations and the decline in the total catch have affected the relationship between Bristol Bay and the entire Alaskan fishery. In the 1930's the monetary value of the Bristol Bay catch was 28 percent of the value of catch for the state (Territory). By the early 1950's, Bristol Bay's share of the total had fallen to 11 percent. But with the sharp increase in the price of red salmon in the late 1950's, it climbed back to 17 percent of the value of the state's catch.

CALCULATION OF POTENTIAL ECONOMIC RENT: BRISTOL BAY

The analysis in Chapter 2 suggests that under open access conditions there will be a tendency to dissipate any net economic rent through new entry and the creation of excess capacity. More and more equipment and more and more men will be used to catch the same number of fish. In spite of the obvious waste in social terms, factors of production will tend to earn, on the average, incomes just sufficient to keep them in the fishery. If factors are highly mobile, these incomes may be equal to those that would be earned in other occupations employing factors of comparable quality. To the extent that it is possible to compute the value of the rent that is dissipated (and if the amount of money involved is significant), the arguments in favor of restrictions on entry and a set of management criteria aimed at optimal factor combinations and time rate of exploitation in economic terms will bear far greater weight.

Ideally, the potential net economic yield would be calculated as follows. On the assumption that total catch is determined administratively by the regulatory authority, the supply function for Bristol Bay red salmon is completely inelastic well above and below the going price. Given the level of market demand, and hence derived demand schedules for raw salmon in separable sub-markets, prices at the fishery level are determined by the catch permitted under regulation. Prices are therefore independent of aggregate fishing costs over a wide range. Rent, a price-determined element of cost, will be zero in equilibrium if entry is free, and any reduction in costs to the individual unit and in the aggregate will simply accrue as explicit or implicit rent.

Calculation of the potential net yield appears to involve no more than a simple comparison of gross receipts to fishermen less minimum attainable total costs. In practice, however, such calculations become treacherous in concept, quite apart from data problems. The definition of minimum attainable costs depends on the extent to which institutional constraints are accepted as given. In the case of the Alaska fisheries generally, traps are clearly the most efficient type of gear where physical conditions permit their use, but in the present political climate there is no possibility that their use will be legalized. Similarly, the attainable yield would be increased very substantially if the present network of efficiency-reducing regulations were dismantled or modified—as they could and probably would be if the number of fishing units could be reduced under regulation. To cite one simple example, the use of monofilament nylon gill nets, now prohibited, would increase the catching power of a boat by as much as 30 percent.

It should also be noted that a more nearly optimal number of fishing units, fishing more continuously, would influence packing costs in several ways. First, reduction in the range of high to low runs would reduce the ratio of peak to average capacity required. Secondly, increased accuracy of forecasting would enable the industry to estimate pre-season planning requirements more correctly and thus to approximate more closely a profit maximizing level of operations.

Estimates of potential net yield from a given salmon fishery are also complicated by the necessity of forecasting future levels of real prices of end products. The simplest (and usually the most defensible) assumption of a constant relative price is manifestly unrealistic in light of the preceding discussion. Some rebuilding of the Alaska stocks is surely possible, but even if they were restored to levels that would support the peak yields of the 1920's and 1930's, they could not keep pace indefinitely with the rightward shifts in demand functions stemming from increases in population and per capita income. The number of imponderables involved in forecasting the magnitude of the increase in real prices of Alaska salmon make it impractical to try, but it should be noted that for this and other reasons subsequent estimates of potential economic rent from the fishery are biased on the low side.

Finally, the calculation of potential net benefits must include consideration of the complexities imposed by the natural biological variability of the run of each race of salmon. At present the ability to predict the size and timing of runs in any given season is severely limited, and we have no real basis for estimating the cost of developing a more adequate forecasting capability. Furthermore, the tendency of the biologist to view any escapement above desired levels as sheer waste leads to the obviously erroneous conclusion that the "minimum number of fishing units required" is the number sufficient to harvest every run fully. The actual optimum involves a complex comparison of the costs of developing more accurate forecasts, the costs of excess capacity—both fishing and processing—and the value of fish "forgone" in the occasional year when runs so far exceed predictions that even full-time fishing and canning operations cannot handle the volume of fish over and above desired escapement levels.[6]

In Bristol Bay the question of traps is not relevant, and the calculation of potential economic yield can be made on the basis of reduction of inputs of the existing type to minimum levels required for harvesting. (We shall assume only the present level

[6] For an analytical summary of these variables and their relation to an optimal research and prediction program, see Stephen B. Mathews, "The Economic Consequences of Forecasting Sockeye Salmon (*Oncorhynchus nerka, Welbaum*) Runs to Bristol Bay, Alaska: A Computer Simulation Study of the Potential Benefits to a Salmon Canning Industry from Accurate Forecasts of the Runs" (unpublished doctoral dissertation, University of Washington, Seattle, Washington, 1966). Mathews makes a strong case for a very high rate of return on "investment in forecasting" in Bristol Bay.

of accuracy of the forecasting program.) The calculation is of considerable significance, since in this one case it is possible to approximate the rent from reasonably comparable realized experience rather than from a purely hypothetical reduction in gear.

The prime requirement is that a base period be available from which relative efficiency in the fishery at other times may be measured; hence, a period in which amounts of inputs, location of fishing effort, and the rate of fishing approximate those that would yield maximum efficiency in the fishery. The years 1942 and 1943 provide an approximation of such a base for analysis of the Bristol Bay fishery. In those years Bristol Bay was in a war zone, and transportation to and from the Bay was extremely difficult. In addition, the proximity of Bristol Bay to the actual conflict provided a reason for relaxing regulatory procedures, especially those affecting the location of the fishing effort. The impact of the restriction on entry and permission to fish closer inshore is reflected in the very sharp increase in yields per unit of input during this base period.

If we assume, first, that the yields per unit of input obtained in 1942 and 1943 represent an approximation of maximum efficiency with existing institutional arrangements (a point that will be discussed in greater detail below), it becomes possible to measure the yield in other years in terms of the 1942–43 base and to develop an index or scale of relative efficiency. A second underlying assumption is that in all other years, at the then current price of fish, all factors earned opportunity incomes.[7]

The calculation of the amount of rent that is dissipated is as follows. The gross earnings of the factors used in each year are known. These are simply the price of fish times the number caught (Bristol Bay fishermen are paid on a per fish basis) or total gross revenue of the fleet. We also know for each year the efficiency, relative to the 1942–43 base, of the fishing fleet. The

---

[7] The qualification for this latter assumption is "in equilibrium." Since the demand function, on the average, was shifting in the period after 1942–43 some rents were included in the opportunity income. The use of five-year averages and the secular rise in fish prices support the reasonableness of this assumption.

index of efficiency makes it possible to estimate, on the basis of 1942–43 yields, the minimum quantity of inputs needed to harvest the number of fish actually caught in any given year.[8] Given the number of units actually required in terms of 1942–43 yields and the assumption of opportunity factor incomes, the difference between the gross earnings of the entire fleet in any year and the gross earnings that would have been required if this fleet had been limited in number and operating at the 1942–43 efficiency level, provides a measure of the potential rent. For example, when the index is at 50 percent, it means that if 2,000 men and 1,000 boats were actually employed, the fishery, operating at 1942–43 levels of efficiency, could have harvested the runs with only 1,000 men and 500 boats. The gross earnings of the 1,000 men and 500 boats that were used, but were not actually necessary, to catch the given year's landings represent the amount of the rent lost in that year.[9] The calculations made for Bristol Bay are as follows (see Tables 4 and 5 for summary).

In 1942 the catch was approximately 6,343,000 fish, and these fish were landed using only 34,355 fathoms of net, a yield of 185

---

[8] This estimation procedure assumes that the yield-to-effort relationship has been constant over the entire period under analysis. There is no way to verify this assumption on the basis of available information. It is possible, of course, that the 1942–43 performance could not be sustained for any very long period because of the cumulative ecological consequences of continuous close inshore fishing. For a similar calculation involving a different fishery, see G. Pontecorvo and K. Vartdal, Jr., "Optimizing Resource Use: The Norwegian Winter Herring Fishery," in *Statsøkonomisk Tidsskrift*, #2, 1967. The results in the Norwegian case are consistent with the Bristol Bay findings. See also N. Farstad and M. Skolnik, "Optimizing Resource Use. The Norwegian Winter Herring Fishery: A Comment," and reply by Pontecorvo and Vartdal, *Statsøkonomisk Tidsskrift*, #3, 1968.

[9] An alternative calculation may be made as a check on this technique. This approach employs data on yields per boat per day that have been taken by the Fisheries Research Institute for the Bay. These yields per boat per day cover the period from 1947 to 1957. They are highly variable, but they are also markedly peaked. In each year there have been periods when the landings per boat were quite high. If we take the highs, that is those days when the boats were landing at or close to the peak number of fish, we also have a rough measure of minimum required capacity of the fleet. These yields divided into the total catch should give us a measure of the number of boats required to land the entire catch and this measure should be consistent with the measure we have derived in the calculation given previously.

Table 4. Fishing Gear in Use in Bristol Bay (Drift Gill Nets Only)

Period	Fathoms of net[a]	Number of boats	Number of men[b]
1934–39[c]	161,850	1,079	2,158
1940–44	83,771	558	1,116
1945–49	106,355	709	1,418
1950–54	124,492	830	1,660
1955–59	114,995	767	1,534
1955–59	172,493[d]	767	1,534

[a] Fathoms of gill net calculated by multiplying number of boats engaged in fishing one year times 150 fathoms/boat and averaging over five-year period.

[b] Number of men engaged in fishery is two per boat.

[c] Year 1935 excluded because of voluntary closure of fishery.

[d] Average for 1955–59 is an adjusted figure that includes a 50 percent allowance for productivity increase (power for sail, etc.). See text.

Source: International North Pacific Salmon Commission, Bulletin No. 10, *The Exploitation Scientific Investigation and Management of Salmon Stocks on the Pacific Coast of North America*, paper No. 11, "Supplementary Information on Salmon Stocks of the United States: Fishing Intensity for Each Type of Gear," 1962.

Table 5. Calculation of Dissipated Rent in Bristol Bay

Period	(A) Efficiency of gear[a]	(B) Relative amount of unnecessary gear[b]	(C) Rent dissipated[c] Current	(C) Rent dissipated[c] Real
	catch/fathom	*percent*	*million dollars*	
1934–39	124	33	0.897	1.850
1940–44	112	40	0.439	0.819
1945–49	103	45	1.125	1.445
1950–54	54	71	1.904	2.184
1955–59	51	75	2.777	3.134
1955–59[d]	32	83	3.506	3.608

[a] Efficiency: catch/year divided by number of fathoms/year and averaged over five-year period.

[b] Optimum efficiency (1942–43) is assumed to be 186 fish/fathom.

[c] Rent dissipated: Col. B times values of catch, in current dollars and in real terms.

[d] Assuming a 50 percent increase in efficiency of gear. See text.

115

fish per fathom. Operating conditions improved somewhat in 1943, when 93,000 fathoms were employed, but the catch jumped to over 17,330,000 fish so that the yield per fathom actually rose to 187 fish. At no other time during the period covered by the data (1934–59) has the catch per fathom approached these figures.[10]

Given this base, which is differentiated both statistically and on an *a priori* basis from the rest of the period, the index of efficiency was computed as a set of simple relatives. For example, in 1938 approximately 8 percent of the gear was redundant, but in 1955, when the yield was only 35 fish per fathom, over 80 percent of the inputs represented excess costs; i.e., if the gear had been used as efficiently as in the base period, only 20 percent of the gear actually used could have landed the entire catch in that year.

The dollar cost of this inefficiency is startling. In 1955 the money value of landings was $2,970,000. This amount, multiplied by the efficiency index, gives $2,412,000 as the amount of rent dissipated in Bristol Bay in that year alone.

One additional adjustment should be made in the index of efficiency. Over the years, regulations have persistently tended to reduce efficiency. These regulations have affected seasonal openings, equipment, and also the area of fishing. Gradually the fishery has been pushed out of and away from the river mouths. By moving the fishing effort from areas of high density of fish to areas of lower density, the efficiency of the individual fishing unit has been reduced.[11]

The pressures to reduce efficiency through the regulatory process have been offset, however, in significant ways. The most

[10] In 1938, the peak year, when almost 25 million fish were taken, the yield per fathom was 152, the second highest total. During the 1950's the range was from 91 to 30 fish per fathom.

[11] As noted earlier, some benefits may accrue from this procedure. If the fish are taken in an area where there is more mixing of various races, the danger of overfishing a particular stock may be reduced, and the increased physical yield, up to some limit, will offset the increase in fishing costs. There may also be some improvement in quality, though in Bristol Bay the difference would not normally be significant.

116

important technological improvement in Bristol Bay came in the 1950's, when fishermen were permitted to shift from sail to motor boats. Today the fishery uses better nets and hauling techniques, and a number of less obvious changes have improved the environment in which the fishermen work and live. Perhaps the most important change has been in the fishermen themselves. The decline in the level of the catch has increased the competition for the remaining fish, and with a steadily increasing proportion of independent fishermen (perhaps two-thirds of the total at present), canneries have become increasingly selective in financing new producers.

No specific weights may be assigned to the various factors that have operated to augment or diminish productivity in the fishery. In the judgment of close observers of the fishery, however, the positive forces have predominated, especially the selectivity mechanism and the transition from sail to power.

Comparisons of the operation of this fishery in the 1930's and the 1950's should reflect this net gain in productivity. A conservative estimate suggests a 50 percent net increase in the efficiency of inputs over two decades as a minimum. Allowance for productivity change, of course, accentuates the difference between actual and attainable yield per unit of gear. The catch per fathom in the period 1955–59, with no allowance for productivity increases, was 51; but with a 50 percent allowance for productivity change, the yield drops to 32. At that level, the overall operation was 17 percent as efficient as in the base period.

Finally, since the gill net fishery operates on the basis of fixed proportions—one net, one boat, and two men—the rent may be described either in the aggregate or in terms of specific inputs. As Table 5 indicates, in the period 1955–59, without any allowance for increased productivity, annual unadjusted money payments to redundant inputs were $2,777,000, or almost 64 percent of the actual value of the fishery. If we recalculate the data to allow for an estimated 50 percent change in productivity, the rent dissipated rises to $3,506,000 per year.

Unfortunately, it is impossible to carry the analysis beyond 1959, since the series indicating actual gear in use was terminated at that time.

OTHER FACTORS AFFECTING EFFICIENCY

These estimates of the amount of rent involved are shocking in themselves, but they do not fully reveal the extent of present inefficiency in the fishery. The marked improvement in the administration of the conservation regulations in the 1950's was accompanied by some adverse effects on economic efficiency. As the catch fell, the regulatory agency was forced to reduce the open fishing time. In the earlier periods, fishing time had been almost unlimited during the season. As indicated above, the actual impact of limitations on fishing time is apt to be ambiguous. The availability of the fish through time is extremely peaked, and there is considerable annual variation in the peaks. This means that restrictions at the beginning or end of the season do not have the same effect as similar closures during the height of the run, and closing dates may or may not have the same impact from year to year.

Regardless of the effectiveness of time closures in reducing catch and improving the chances of achieving desired escapement, they tend to add to the cost of fishing. Average total fishing time in the Bay fell from slightly below 20 days in the 1930's and 1940's to 12 days per year in the later 1950's, thus reducing by 40 percent the exposure time of the gear without commensurate reductions in capital and other costs. In recent years the adjustments in fishing time, area by area, have been defined in terms of hours, with further adjustments for tidal conditions. The resulting complexities may permit more precise management of the individual runs, but obviously add to economic costs.

The improvement in federal and, subsequently, state administration of the fishery brought increasing awareness of the integral nature of the economic and biological problems facing the fishery, and of the dangers inherent in excess fishing capacity. The possibility of effective action was limited, however, for two reasons. First, there was no legal authority to restrict entry, and every tradition and public attitude toward the fisheries in Alaska would have opposed the idea. Secondly, the absence of an adequate analytical base for a policy of restricted entry meant that no consistent attack on the problem could be launched, despite the fact that the need for restriction of fishing effort was obvious to all careful observers. In fact, since the entire structure of biological regulations was threatened by the growth of fishing capacity, certain administrative techniques were adopted that were designed to reduce the increasingly dangerous pressure on the fishery.

The first of these could be characterized as "moral suasion." The combination of the declining runs and the marked improvement in the sophistication of forecasting the runs lent strength to this approach. The industry was under pressure to reduce overhead costs, and the increased accuracy of the forecasts provided a rationale for some limited steps in this direction.

The Bureau of Commercial Fisheries also carried out some studies on yield per unit of effort during this period and those studies became the basis for a relatively simple area control plan.[12] The Bay was divided into four districts. Prior to each week's fishing, it was necessary to register gear for use in the coming week in each district. With the amount of gear fixed for each district in each time period, the intensity of fishing effort could be regulated quite closely by adjusting the exposure time (i.e., fishing time) allowed. Naturally this regulatory procedure of cutting down on fishing time reduces the secular decline in yields per fathom day.

Instituting this kind of regulation is also important for other reasons. It represents a significant improvement in technique with respect to physical control. Unfortunately, the same is not true of its effects on costs. In spite of the obvious adroitness of the regulatory procedures (introduced in the face of general opposition to *any* change), they failed to solve the basic problem of economic efficiency. The solution adopted—the reduction of exposure time of inputs—was a step in the wrong direction. An optimum solution must first limit inputs and then work to increase the productivity of each input. The techniques discussed above not only increase fishing costs per unit of catch, but also require much heavier administrative and enforcement costs than

[12] The Myren Report, unpublished and undated manuscript. Bureau of Commercial Fisheries, Juneau, Alaska.

would be necessary if most of the excess capacity were removed rather than throttled.

QUALIFICATIONS

The final step in evaluation of the efficiency problem in Bristol Bay is to enumerate some qualifications to the basic argument presented. The first and most important of these involves the adequacy of the base period used. It is clear that in 1942–43 entry was restricted and there was a marked relaxation in the degree of efficiency–reducing regulation imposed upon the fishery. Apart from the reduction in fishing units, the most important change was to allow fishermen to operate closer inshore than had been the case under ordinary conditions. While not perfect, the 1942–43 period does appear defensible as an approximation to an optimal fishery for the situation then prevailing.

Available data are not adequate to answer the obvious question as to the appropriateness of the fishing capacity available in 1942–43. As indicated earlier, the ideal capacity would involve balancing at the margin the value of escaping fish in excess of desired spawners against the cost of maintaining full harvesting capacity *over time*. The calculation is made more difficult, even under the most favorable circumstances, by the pronounced (and variable) peaking of the Bristol Bay runs. It can be argued, with reasonable confidence, that the capacity in 1942–43 was more likely to be above the optimum than below. For this reason, as well as those enumerated earlier, the estimates of potential rent are conservative.[13]

In the past, efforts at regulation have been directed toward reducing the efficiency of individual units. This has taken the form of direct prohibition of the use of certain techniques and equipment, the imposition of time limits on the use of equipment, and the use of registration techniques that prevent shifting of equipment from one area to another within seasons. Given this orientation toward inefficiency, there is little real knowledge

[13] Similarly, Mathews' estimates of the potential net economic benefits from improved accuracy of the biological forecast of the runs suggest further realizable increases in net economic yield not accounted for in our crude measures.

120

of what may be called the efficiency potential. No one ever investigated the fishery from the point of view of maximizing technological efficiency in harvesting the fish. The fishery is in dire need of engineering efficiency studies of all kinds to determine the optimum design of boats and gear as well as the appropriate number of units. If the fishery were put on a rational basis, the rate of productivity increase, even in the short run, could be very marked, and the potential net yield would again exceed the estimates outlined above.

CHAPTER 8

The Puget Sound Case:
Background and History

~~~~~~

The Puget Sound salmon fishery is based on annual runs of five species of mature salmon that pass through the Strait of Juan de Fuca and Puget Sound on their way from ocean feeding grounds to spawning areas on the coast of Washington and British Columbia. Virtually all of the sockeye or red salmon taken in this fishery spawn in the Fraser River system; all of the others—pink, chum, coho, and chinook—originate in other rivers emptying into Puget Sound as well as the Fraser. The fish are taken along their entire migration route in both Canadian and U.S. waters (see Map 2). In addition, chinook and coho salmon are subjected to an intensive troll fishery in the open ocean and at the mouth of the Strait of Juan de Fuca. Chinook and coho salmon (and, to a lesser extent, the pinks) are also the object of a major sport fishery extending from the ocean feeding grounds throughout the Strait of Juan de Fuca and Puget Sound areas. The fishery is characterized by a peculiar annual distribution of the runs. Although the sockeye and pink salmon are the most important species, the latter is available only in odd-numbered years. For reasons not clear to biologists, no runs can be expected in even-

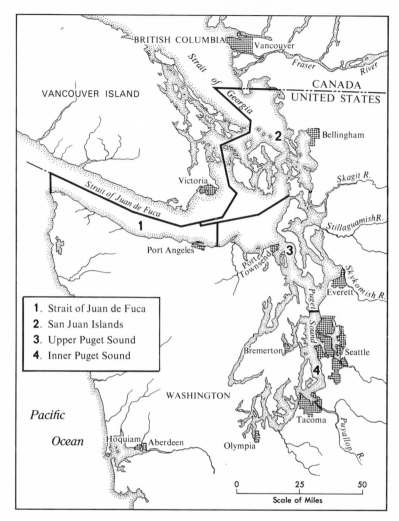

BRITISH COLUMBIA Vancouver
Fraser River
CANADA
VANCOUVER ISLAND
UNITED STATES
Strait of Georgia
Bellingham
2
Victoria
Skagit R.
Strait of Juan de Fuca
1
Stillaguamish R.
Port Angeles
Port Townsend
3
Skykomish R.
Everett
Puget Sound
1. Strait of Juan de Fuca
2. San Juan Islands
3. Upper Puget Sound
4. Inner Puget Sound
Bremerton
Seattle
4
WASHINGTON
Pacific
Tacoma
Puyallop R.
Ocean Hoquiam Aberdeen Olympia
0   25   50
Scale of Miles

Map 2. Major Fishing Areas in U.S. Waters of Puget Sound and Strait of Juan de Fuca. Source: Department of Fisheries, State of Washington.

numbered years despite intensive efforts to establish them in rivers that produce excellent catches in odd years.

The conditions under which the various species of salmon enter the commercial fishery and move through to their spawning streams play a major part in determination of the activities of both the industry and the regulatory agencies. The Puget Sound

123

fishery, like that of Alaska, is confined to a limited period of time in each of the areas through which the fish pass. One factor of major concern is the variability in timing of the peaks of the runs in the various fishing areas. The time of entry into the fishery and subsequent peak runs in the several regulatory areas may vary by several weeks from year to year. This is caused in part by fluctuations in oceanographic conditions and in part by the complex racial composition of some major species. Though all of the sockeye are Fraser River fish, for example, the "Fraser River run" actually comprises a number of distinct stocks or races that spawn in the five major lake systems, and a larger number of minor ones within the Fraser River drainage. Since each of these races has its own migration pattern, variations in the relative size of each group alter the timing of the run as a whole. Fluctuations in the timing of the other species are even greater, since they depend not only on Fraser River fish but on those of many other spawning streams spread over a rather wide geographic area. Similar variations exist in the time of travel through the Strait and Puget Sound areas and—most important—the estuarine areas at the mouths of the spawning streams.

The significance of these variations, which collectively can produce very substantial deviations from mean values, is accentuated by the dispersion of fishing gear over the entire area in question. Three major types of gear are employed—purse seines, gill nets, and reef nets. Since the different types of gear are most effective under different conditions, they are typically fished in overlapping but somewhat separate sub-areas. Consequently, variations in the timing of arrival of runs, and in travel time through the fishery, will alter the composition of the catch by gear and the aggregate technical efficiency of the combined fleets.

The relatively long exposure, geographically and temporally, of the salmon to the Puget Sound fishery and the multinational character of the industry lend particular importance to the matters of timing discussed above. There are, of course, the same wide variations in the size of the runs around expected values and the tendency for cyclical peaks and troughs to perpetuate themselves, already noted in the discussion of the Alaska salmon industry. And these impose the same heavy burdens on both the industry—at fishing, processing, and marketing levels—and the regulatory authority.

In several important respects the setting of the Puget Sound salmon fishery gives rise to different problems, for both industry and regulatory authority, than those of Alaska. From the very outset the salmon industry has faced a formidable set of competing water users in rivers, estuaries, and bays. The activities of the forest products industries and agriculture, and the concentration of rural and urban populations along the spawning rivers and at their mouths, have altered the ecology of the Puget Sound river systems in a host of ways, most of them detrimental to the highly sensitive salmonids. While only a few of the rivers involved have yet been developed for hydroelectric power production, some flood control projects have been undertaken that have also contributed to the decline of the salmon runs. The most serious effect, according to competent biologists, has been the relentless destruction of small spawning creeks by urban construction and the rising tide of municipal and industrial pollution.

Apart from the discouraging portent of these factors for the long-run future of the salmon runs, they complicate enormously the research effort required to link fishing effort to long-term productivity. At our present (and prospective) levels of knowledge, it is simply impossible to disentangle the separate effects of changes in habitat and environment and changes in the level and composition of fishing effort on the salmon stocks of Puget Sound and the Fraser River system.

Regulation of the Puget Sound fishery is also complicated, to a much greater degree than in Alaska, by the competition among the predominant net fishery, on the one hand, and the burgeoning ocean troll and sport fisheries on the other. While this competition involves in effect only chinook and silver salmon (some pinks are taken by trollers and sportsmen, but not in large numbers), it is becoming increasingly important in both economic and political terms. The full ramifications of these conflicts are explored in the recommendations in Chapter 9. The essential point for this portion of our analysis is that neither troll nor sport fishery is subject to effective regulation;[1] both are growing rapidly relative to the net fishery; and both catch or destroy large numbers of salmon that are probably "immature" in the economic sense (i.e., fish that would grow rapidly if left for another year with less than offsetting losses from natural mortality).

Of the two, the troll fishery probably presents the more serious "open end" to management. There is no effective control over total effort, and because present regulatory policy militates against landing of net-caught fish of suitable quality for the fresh and frozen market, further expansion of the troller fleet is encouraged. As pointed out in Chapter 3, the trolling operation is inherently wasteful in that it catches fish too soon, injures or kills immatures below legal size, and severely reduces the ability to manage, as separate units, the stocks intermingled on the trolling grounds.

The Puget Sound fishery was developed only slightly earlier than that of Alaska, and the subsequent pattern of governmental action differed only in details and in the greater weight attached to international considerations. One finds no real support for methodical scientific research and the accumulation of relevant knowledge as a basis for regulatory activity until the late 1930's and 1940's at the earliest. Yet the evidence of depletion in the Puget Sound fisheries was plain to see long before that time. The chinook catch reached 477,000 fish in 1918, then went into a long decline which has continued virtually uninterrupted ever since. The largest catch of chums was made in 1914, although the decline that has reached critical proportions in recent years did not begin until the 1930's. Similarly, the greatest catch of silver salmon was recorded in 1918 and the pink and sockeye salmon catches peaked several years earlier. It must have been apparent by 1920 (and probably before that time) that serious damage could be and apparently had been done to some salmon stocks, and that there was urgent need for joint action with Canada on the dominant Fraser River runs. Yet agreement was not reached

[1] The troll fishery is subject to a closed season and a minimum size limit. Sport fishermen face only a minimum size limit and a daily (but not total) catch limit.

*Fig. 12. Puget Sound: Fishing intensity and salmon catch, 1935–61.
Source: Department of Fisheries, State of Washington. Index based
on data series discontinued after 1961.*

until 1937, and effective regulations based on the subsequent
research date only from 1946.

For reasons discussed below, it is impossible to develop accurate measures of fishing capacity prior to World War II. The
dismal story of the development of the salmon fishery in Puget
Sound after World War II is clearly illustrated, however, in
Figure 12. This index of fishing intensity is based on data developed in the course of a study of the Puget Sound fishery con-
ducted by the University of Washington in 1963,[2] and uses pro-

[2] W. Royce, D. Bevan, J. Crutchfield, G. Paulik, and R. Fletcher, *Salmon
Gear Limitation in Northern Washington Waters,* University of Washington
Publications in Fisheries, New Series, Vol II, No. 1, 1963.

ductivity weights to reduce the three major types of gear used— gill nets, purse seines, and reef nets—to a standard fishing unit. The picture portrayed by Figure 12 is strikingly similar to that of Alaska. Despite stable landings of some species and steady declines in landings of others, the level of fishing capacity has expanded in spectacular fashion. The reasons for this have been discussed thoroughly in preceding chapters; its implications for economic performance of the Puget Sound industry are analyzed in Chapter 9.

INDUSTRY STRUCTURE

Since Puget Sound salmon are not differentiated, in an economic sense, from those packed in other areas, the concentration ratios for sellers of canned salmon discussed in Chapter 4 are equally applicable to Alaska and Puget Sound.

The market for raw fish is very similar to that of southeastern Alaska. The same species are involved; most of the catch is taken with the same types of gear (purse seines and gill nets); and many vessels, particularly in the seine fleet, fish in both areas. As indicated in Table 6, concentration among buyers is about the same as in southeastern Alaska. During the past decade, mergers have increased the relative position of the four largest firms in Puget Sound as well as in Alaska. As indicated in Chapter 4, however, the motives for the consolidation movement are clearly linked to the general decline in output and to the consequent search for the least painful method of disinvestment and for reduction of risk through diversification of sources of supply, rather than to any drive to control prices through restriction of output.

There are still no effective barriers to entry to the Puget Sound industry other than the shortage of fish, and the number of participants has remained large enough to produce even more instability in fish buying practices than in Alaska. Excess capacity has been chronic in the processing sector for the past two decades, and the desperate struggle to obtain sufficient fish to keep unit costs within reason has been a major factor in the senseless increase in fishing units on Puget Sound waters.

The competitive situation that developed has had a most unfortunate effect on the economic structure of the fishery. As fish

Table 6. Concentration Ratios: Puget Sound Salmon Canners

(percent of total)

Item	1954	1955	1956	1957	1958	1959	1960	1961	1962	1963	1964	1965
First four firms	41	39	37	37	43	36	38	39	40	50	58	58
First eight firms	65	69	56	63	70	61	61	61	62	78	88	82

Source: M. E. Rubinstein, "The History of Concentration in the Canned Salmon Industry of the United States" (unpublished Bachelor's thesis, Harvard University, 1966), Appendix A.

became increasingly scarce, there was a steady drift toward closer financial ties between canners and individual fishing vessel owners. The disastrous effects on cannery operations of an insufficient supply of fish are so clear that the marginal cost to any one canner of acquiring additional fish by various open and concealed payments to individual vessel owners appears considerably lower than the increment to revenue realized by putting a larger number of fish through the plant. In these circumstances the canner who loses a vessel to a rival has two options: he can "steal" another vessel from some other canner; or he can underwrite the outfitting of a new boat to be fished by one of his own share fishermen (or anyone else who can be persuaded to operate the vessel), thus restoring his share of the total catch.

REGULATION OF THE PUGET SOUND FISHERY: INTRODUCTION

Any survey of regulations affecting the salmon fishery of the Puget Sound must be limited to major actions, since their complexity has mounted to stifling proportions in recent years. As with all fishery regulation, the mass of detail cloaks effectively the initial purposes and makes it extraordinarily difficult to delineate any thread of continuity or philosophical basis for management, let alone any clear evidence of a search for relevant scientific knowledge of the resource. It is important, nevertheless, to trace the development of the present regulatory framework not only in terms of actions taken, but also in terms of avowed objectives and, where possible, the hidden purposes not immediately evident in the legislation itself.

Four separate periods can be distinguished. From 1890 to 1921 legislation regulating salmon fishing was largely limited to establishment of closed seasons and the banning of some types of gear from spawning rivers of the state. The history of the period indicates no particular understanding, nor even a consistent theory, of the parameters determining the life history of the Pacific salmon. As best we can determine from the dim record, most of the regulations promulgated in the state of Washington were based on an intuitive feeling that certain types of gear were excessively destructive, or were undertaken in response to the interests of one pressure group or another.

130

The second period began in 1921 with the establishment in Washington of a Department of Fisheries and a Fisheries Board, and terminated with the major revision in regulatory philosophy that came into being in 1935 as a result of the famous Initiative 77.[3]

From 1935 to 1946 the regulatory process consisted essentially of consolidation of regulations and adaptation of both the fishery and the management program to the technological shifts brought about by Initiative 77. The final period began in 1946 with the issuance of the first regulations by the International Pacific Salmon Fisheries Commission. Work of the Commission was extended to the pink salmon runs of the Fraser River and various Puget Sound streams in 1957, at which point a substantial proportion of the total catch of the Puget Sound area, by weight and value, was brought under international regulation.

It should be borne in mind that the salmon fisheries of Puget Sound were, from the outset, subject to the jurisdiction of the state of Washington, since the catching operation is clearly intrastate in character. The creation of an international regulatory commission—an essential step if the multinational fishery were to be managed at all—was long delayed and its eventual organizational form strongly influenced by the insistence on the primacy of the state's interest. The political battles that arose over salmon management policies and techniques were no less bitter in Puget Sound than in Alaska, but the focal points of the conflicts reflected these differences in the jurisdictional as well as the physical environment of the fishery.

REGULATION BEFORE 1921

Regulation of the salmon fishery prior to 1921 was undertaken directly by the legislature of the state of Washington. But there was no technical staff to guide the legislature, nor does the record suggest that its deliberations were based on more than a cursory knowledge of the life history of the Pacific salmon. It does not appear that regulations were influenced in any significant way by the work of the few scientists then interested in salmon research.

Details of the development of regulation during this period

[3] See p. 137 for details of this action.

may be summarized briefly as follows. The principal techniques of regulation consisted of limited time closures; progressively more stringent limitations on fixed gear of various types; and restrictions on the use of salmon fishing gear of any type in the rivers. The most significant development during the latter part of the period prior to 1921 was the delineation of more and more areas subject to closure, limitations on fishing time, and restrictions on types of gear permitted. It should also be noted that a minimum size limit was imposed for the first time in 1913.

1921 TO 1935

The history of salmon regulation in Puget Sound really begins with the creation of the Washington State Department of Fisheries in 1921. The new department consisted of a Fisheries Board, a Division of Fisheries, and a Division of Game and Game Fish. The director of the new department took over the duties of the commissioner, and the Fisheries Board undertook the task of drawing up the regulations governing the fisheries of the state. The duties of the Fisheries Board as outlined by the legislature were as follows:

> The State Fisheries Board shall have the power to investigate the habits, supply, and economic use of, and to classify, the food fishes in the waters of the State of Washington and, from time to time, make, adopt, amend, and promulgate rules and regulations governing the taking thereof, (1) fixing the times when the taking of the several classes of, and all, food fishes is prohibited, (2) specifying and defining the place and waters in which the taking of the several classes of, and all, food fishes is prohibited, and (3) defining, fixing and prescribing the kind of gear, appliances, or other means that may be used in taking the several classes of food fishes, and the times, places, and manner of using the same.[4]

The hopes and expectations underlying the creation of the Fisheries Board are best illustrated by the words of two influential figures who had much to do with its establishment: L. H. Darwin, State Commissioner of Fisheries, and Miller Freeman, editor of the authoritative trade journal *Pacific Fisherman*.

[4] Session Laws of the State of Washington, *Administrative Code* (1921), 17th Sess., c. 7, sec. 110, p. 59.

In an editorial in the *Pacific Fisherman*,[5] Miller Freeman supported the formation of the Board because he felt that it could meet emergencies as they arose since the Board would not have to wait for the meeting of a large body like the legislature. Thus regulations would be based on "expert knowledge and investigation rather than political expediency." L. H. Darwin wanted the change, to use his own words, because: "My experience led me to the conclusion that it would be impossible to preserve the fisheries of this state through legislative enactment. This for the reason that selfishly interested parties had always theretofore succeeded and would likely thereafter succeed in so confusing the legislature as to prevent the passage of any real conservation measures."[6] It might be noted, parenthetically, that as of 1968 this problem is still in the center of the stage.

The significance of the new Fisheries Board was more a matter of approach than of administration. For the first time there was official recognition of the fact that salmon conservation required use and extension of scientific data. That its efforts were frequently frustrated is all too apparent from a summation by Edward P. Blake at the end of a hearing in Seattle in 1923. The statement is a reasonably good indication of the state of knowledge at the time, and of the bases for "conservation" actions.

As I explained briefly to you in our little conference before the hearing commenced, the state, as a state, has made no provision for the activities of this Board. If the Board desires to act intelligently on these questions, it has got to get information. It is unreasonable to assume that any three men picked at random would be familiar with a subject that scientists have given years of study to and still accomplished very little. You can read any of the trade papers or journals that make reference to fishing, that the United States authorities—and I think that Mr. Watson will bear me out in that—are at sea on this proposition.

Now, we tried to create a sentiment in this state that the fishing industry of the state of Washington was worth caring for. That we failed utterly is evident by the attitude of the legislature, because they made no provision whatever for the fish feature of this state. It is true

5 February 1921, p. 34.
6 *Thirtieth and Thirty-first Annual Reports of the State Fish Commission to the Governor of the State of Washington* (Olympia, 1921), p. 9.

they did pass the budget that this Board filed, which covers purely the office expenses, with no provision in the budget for anything else. We anticipated at that time that provision would be made for the activities of the Board so that they could accomplish something. But the budget for propagation and development and rehabilitation of the salmon industry was absolutely cut out.

Now you can readily understand this Board individually has got a living to make, the same as you gentlemen have; we can't go up and down the streams and back and forth in this country, finding out things that ought to be found out. The state makes no provision for it, and I think that I will not be challenged when I make this statement, that no assistance has been rendered this Board by any phase of the industry. All that we have come in contact with is exactly what we have come in contact with today—objections to our policy, a policy that was founded upon such information as we were able to gather.

Now, you gentlemen are simply typical of the whole industry. You are interested in a particular phase of it, yet I don't think there is anyone here who has made any effort whatever to learn concerning conditions, learn what was necessary to do, who has favored the Board with any information on any subject whatever. Now, I am not criticizing you for that because it seems to be universal. The people of the state of Washington apparently do not want fish.[7]

The following statement from one of the leading scientists of the day is also illustrative, in a different manner, of the primitive state of knowledge of the complex life history of the salmon during the period in which the basic framework of both the fishery and its regulation was laid down.

We are now reasonably certain that the vast majority of the salmon are comparatively near our coastline, while others stay in the bays, straits, and sounds virtually all the time when not in the rivers.[8]

The frontiers of knowledge were being pushed back in this period, and since Washington State and British Columbia shared a common fishery there were two independent bodies engaged in research which was readily available to all—the College of Fisheries of the University of Washington, in Seattle, and a branch of the Fisheries Research Board of Canada at Nanaimo, British

[7] Statement made by Edward P. Blake, *Washington State Fisheries Board Hearing* (1923), No. 1. This hearing was held in Seattle on April 28, 1923, and the report is available at the Fisheries Oceanography Library, University of Washington, Seattle, Washington.

[8] John Cobb in the *Pacific Fisherman* (July 1920), p. 3.

Columbia. By 1925 Cobb's surmise was challenged when scientists at Nanaimo successfully tagged king and silver salmon on both sides of Vancouver Island in northern British Columbia which were later taken in the Fraser, the Skagit, and some Oregon rivers. Indeed, much of the subsequent period was characterized by demolition of accepted ideas as the biological knowledge of the resource accumulated. Finally in 1958 Canadian scientists reported to a meeting of the International North Pacific Fisheries Commission in Tokyo that Fraser River sockeye had been found as far west as 155 degrees west longitude.

As in Alaska, the operations of the regulatory authority in Washington during the 1920's and early 1930's were strongly influenced by the belief (or wish) that man's predation on the salmon fishery could be fully compensated by fish hatcheries. The Fisheries Board, observing that most runs of salmon were being further depleted despite hatchery operations, viewed the problem as a choice between two alternatives: (1) there were not enough hatcheries, and to get an adequate number might involve excessive cost; (2) there was not enough escapement to maintain or increase natural propagation. The Board chose to emphasize the latter by concentrating on increased escapement.

This approach was not popular in all quarters. Those who profited from the industry could hardly be expected to look with relish on any program that asked them to reduce the catch. Existing knowledge of the resource provided no clear assurance that a sacrifice on their part would be rewarded with larger catches in later years. Furthermore, with respect to the fish of the Fraser River, American fishermen feared, not unreasonably, that what they allowed to escape would simply be taken by Canadian fishermen.

There was, moreover, sharp disagreement among recognized fishery scientists as to the efficiency of hatcheries in a salmon enhancement program. John Cobb wrote in the *Pacific Fisherman*:[9]

When reproached with their shortsightedness [fishermen and packers] clamored for the establishment of more salmon hatcheries, as though the

[9] December 1921, p. 5.

latter could accomplish the miracle of increasing the supply of fry from a steadily decreasing supply of eggs.

The decreasing supply of eggs was a vital consideration, because as the runs thinned out fewer fish were available to the hatcheries for stripping. In 1930 Cobb sharpened his attack when he referred to "an idolatrous faith in the efficacy of artificial culture for replenishing the ravages of man and animals." In 1920 Dr. Evermann pointed out in an address to a meeting of Pacific Fisheries Societies that hatcheries had consistently failed to maintain runs.[10]

On the other hand, hatchery operations were vigorously championed by R. E. Clanton, an Oregon fish culturist, and Dr. Charles H. Gilbert. Clanton had made a survey of the Fraser River spawning grounds and recommended the construction of rearing ponds in addition to other measures for the reconstruction of depleted runs of sockeye. It was argued that these ponds would minimize the loss from natural enemies on spawning grounds. Gilbert's support of hatcheries rested largely on the proposition that natural spawning as a means of rebuilding the depleted sockeye runs would be a "slow and tedious process" since only about 1/10 of 1 percent of eggs naturally spawned would return as adults.[11]

The Fisheries Board carried on until 1927. It had been criticized, its constitutionality questioned and tested in court, and some of its regulations rendered inoperative while litigation was under way. It withstood these attacks, usually with the firm support of the *Pacific Fisherman* (and, presumably, some significant part of the industry), but resigned in a body in 1927 after a disagreement concerning a conflict over gear in northern Puget Sound.

Most contemporary observers felt that the Fisheries Board had done good work. It had accomplished little to restore the crucial Fraser River runs, but the pace of depletion was perceptibly slowed in Puget Sound as a whole. The *Pacific Fisherman* commented in 1927 that the Fisheries Board "did more for the fishery than anything in the history of the industry . . . they devoted

[10] *Pacific Fisherman*, July 1920, p. 23.
[11] *Ibid.*, December 1921, pp. 10–11.

themselves earnestly to their task, without compensation and without thanks."[12]

That so little was really accomplished is less an indictment of the Board than a reflection of the fact that the basic problems were not organizational and could not be resolved on the basis of the meager evidence available. The Board possessed no scientific staff or budget to employ outside scientists. It could weigh conflicting claims and pressures only by "feel and common sense," and admirable as these attributes may be, they do not provide a basis for a management program that would inevitably require sound documentation to defend unpopular measures.

It is hardly surprising, then, that this phase of salmon regulation in Puget Sound ended in an abortive series of struggles over gear competition that culminated in a drastic revision of the whole program by initiative.

1935 TO 1946

This phase of the Puget Sound salmon program was ushered in by passage of the famous Initiative 77, the effects of which are still felt. The story of gear warfare is an old one in the fishery industry and the state of Washington is no exception. The principal feature of Initiative 77 was that it eliminated fixed gear (traps, fish wheels, and set nets) from the salmon fishery of the state. In addition, Puget Sound was divided into two areas by Line 77, with severe restrictions on commercial net fishing in the inner area.[13]

Briefly, "outside Line 77" included the Strait of Juan de Fuca and the Strait of Georgia; "inside Line 77" included Puget Sound, Bellingham Bay and the waters of Deception Pass, and south of that area. Initiative 77 also redefined legal fishing gear and closed areas. (See Map 3 for location of Line 77 and closed areas as of April 1965.)

[12] *Ibid.*, June 1927, p. 16.
[13] This line extended from Angeles Point to Point Partridge and overland to intersect Longitude Line 122° 4' west (near the entrance to Penn Cove); thence north along this line to the south shore of Sinclair Island, and from Carter Point on Sinclair Island to the south shore end of Lummi Island; thence north again along the above named longitude line from the north side of Lummi Island to the mainland.

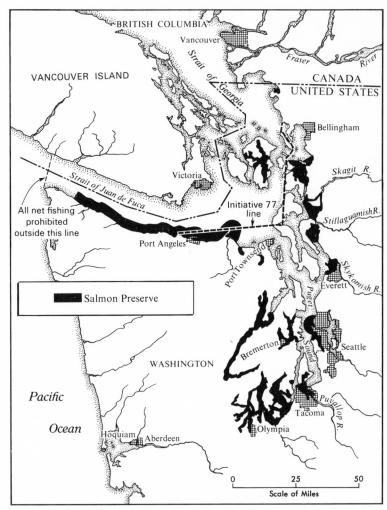

Map 3. *Puget Sound commercial salmon preserves. Source: Department of Fisheries, State of Washington.*

As noted above, gear warfare has a long history. The problem was described by John Cobb in 1910 in a statement that applies with equal force today.

While all forms of apparatus in use in the salmon fishery of the Pacific Coast have been objected to in some one section or another, the principal complaints have been against fish wheels and traps or pound nets. To the objections of other fishermen, the owners of wheels and traps retaliate by charging prejudice and self-interest, and with some justification. It is unquestioned that those costly forms of apparatus are beyond the financial means of the ordinary fishermen, that their use reduces the number of persons employed in the fisheries, and that the owners, who are usually the packers or others closely affiliated with them, can, if they so desire, render themselves largely independent of other fishermen, such as gill netters and seiners, and thus keep down the cost of fish to the packers. Although not often advocated publicly, the objectives are based upon higher grounds, such as the waste through catching and killing in wheels and traps of enormous quantities of salmon which cannot be handled in the limited time available, or of species which the packers have no use for, and which they find it easier or less expensive to kill by much handling than to release and in so doing lose a few salmon.

One thing should never be lost sight of, however: fishery apparatus is set for the purpose of catching fish, and its value is dependent upon the degree of effectiveness with which it accomplishes the object sought with the least expenditure of money and time for construction and operation.[14]

The problem of pressures from owners of competing gear was also faced by the Fisheries Board referred to above. At the close of hearings held in 1921, E. A. Sims, then chairman of the Board, pointed out that the regulations in force at that time resulted in the use of more gear than was necessary. He favored fixed gear because it made it possible to determine escapement while movable gear made this more difficult.[15] While it is easy to overdo the wisdom of the past in hindsight, it is still noteworthy that a few observers of the Puget Sound fisheries, like Gilbert and O'Malley or Rich and Ball in Alaska, were at least dimly aware of the economic origin of the conservation problem and the consequences of neglecting it.

An indication of the extremes to which such movements can go and of the justifications for them is given by a gear controversy of 1924. An initiative was circulated for signatures which would have outlawed all gear in the salt and fresh water salmon fishery of the state except gill nets and trolled lines. Proponents of the

[14] John Cobb, "Salmon Fisheries of the Pacific Ocean." Appendix in the *Report of the U.S. Commissioner of Fisheries*, 1910.
[15] E. A. Sims, *Washington State Fisheries Board Hearing* (1921), p. 107. This hearing was held in Seattle on June 20, 1921.

measure argued that it would allow everyone in the state to fish for salmon, "thereby giving employment to more than 10,000 additional citizens of the state."[16] The next step, presumably, would have been to outlaw the use of boats. Fortunately, the measure failed to get on the ballot.

Throughout the 1920's and 1930's, constant efforts were being made to win ratification of a treaty between Canada and the United States for management of the Fraser River sockeye. Initiative 77 and its effects on the sockeye catch in Puget Sound inadvertently provided much of the impetus needed to achieve agreement. Prior to 1935, the Washington catch exceeded that of British Columbia. After 1935, however, this was reversed. In 1936, the British Columbia catch was more than triple that of Puget Sound. The treaty was ratified in 1937.

The repercussions of Initiative 77 were to continue to the present. It set the stage for a long series of regulations designed specifically to reduce economic efficiency as a means of protecting salmon stocks or having important secondary effects of this nature. It completely disrupted the pattern of the Puget Sound fishery as mobile gear made its way into the areas formerly dominated by the traps and, in so doing, created a discontinuity in catch and effort statistics that makes it almost impossible to tie pre-1935 to post-1935 data.

The International Pacific Salmon Fisheries
Commission: 1946

Although these periods have been arranged in consecutive order, there is no clear cleavage in fact between the conceptual periods in the regulations dealing with the salmon fishery. So it is with the period 1946–67. The salient feature was the creation and maturing of the international program for regulation of the Fraser River fishery, but efforts to negotiate such a treaty date back almost to the turn of the century. An international study of the Fraser River sockeye was undertaken in 1892. The first treaty was actually drafted in 1908, and while it is tempting to relate the story of the many attempts which were made to obtain ratification and the various ways in which they were frustrated, it is

16 *Pacific Fisherman*, June 1924, p. 12.

140

not essential to our basic argument. Suffice it to say that most of the arguments against curtailment of catch and in favor of hatcheries or other "painless" solutions to the problem of depletion discussed in the Alaska controversies were echoed on Puget Sound. In addition, the crucial question of division of the catch between the nationals of two countries probably delayed the treaty even after agreement on the need for regulation was accepted. In the light of the scientific evidence that was produced by the Commission, the treaty which was finally ratified seems, in retrospect, to have been the most reasonable that could be achieved.[17]

The treaty creating the International Pacific Salmon Fisheries Commission, as ratified in 1937, included three substantive provisions.

(1) The International Pacific Salmon Fisheries Commission would have no power to authorize any fishing contrary to the laws of the state of Washington or Canada.

(2) The International Pacific Salmon Fisheries Commission would not promulgate or enforce regulations until the scientific investigation provided for by the convention was made, covering two cycles of sockeye salmon, or eight years.

(3) The International Pacific Salmon Fisheries Commission would set up an advisory committee composed of five persons from each country who would represent various branches of the industry, and who would be invited to non-executive meetings, with a right to examine all proposed orders, regulations, or recommendations.

From a management point of view, two governing objectives, one long- and one short-term, were to guide the Commission:

(1) The restoration of the Fraser River sockeye runs. Most of the regulations were directed to that end until 1958, when pink salmon were also brought under the Commission's jurisdiction.

---

[17] For the full text of the treaty, as amended to 1965, with additional commentary, see *Treaties and Other International Agreements Containing Provisions on Commercial Fisheries, Marine Resources, Sport Fisheries and Wildlife to which the United States is a Party*, A Report Prepared for the Committee on Commerce, U.S. Senate, by Legislative Reference Service, Library of Congress, January 1965, pp. 214–38.

(2) An equal division of the catch, within practical limits, between Canadian and American fishermen.

The first three features appeared to be concessions to the hard core of resistance in Washington to the ratification of any treaty. The last two were permanent features of the structure created under the treaty.

The Commission was given relatively wide powers with respect to the underlying scientific work to be done. It was empowered to investigate the natural history of the salmon, especially the spawning ground environment, and to employ its own staff to do so. It could conduct operations designed to improve spawning grounds, remove obstructions to migration, and operate hatcheries. It was empowered to limit or prohibit the taking of sockeye by stipulating seasons when sockeye could be taken, and by stipulating legal size of mesh in all fishing gear during open seasons and during closed seasons when sockeye might be taken incidentally to other species.[18]

The scientific orientation of the International Pacific Salmon Fisheries Commission in both research and regulatory operations marked a clear break with the past and laid the groundwork for increasingly solid support from industry and governmental personnel. Its first achievement was the discovery of and solution of the block to migration at Hell's Gate in the Fraser River. There was general agreement after 1921 that the slide of 1913 had been removed; that salmon could pass; and that only adequate escapement was needed to restore the sockeye runs. The Commission's early investigations made it clear there was a loss of escaped fish somewhere in the Fraser River system. In 1941 it was learned that the block was at Hell's Gate, and that its devastating effects oper-

---

[18] Technically, the Commission has no power to enforce limits on fishing; it can only recommend such actions to the Canadian Department of Fisheries and the Department of Fisheries of the state of Washington. In practice, however, the recommendations, once promulgated, have always been implemented by both governments. The treaty specifies the matters on which recommendations can be made, and prohibits the authorization of any type of gear proscribed by legislation of the state of Washington or of Canada (marine fisheries in Canada are under the jurisdiction of the federal, rather than provincial, government).

ated only at certain water levels. In 1942 a power brailer was put into operation to elevate the fish below the Gate and they were then sluiced into calmer waters above the Gate. Eventually 15 fishways were constructed, at a total cost of $2 million. Subsequent development of a wide range of "pro-fish" research and management activities brought the Fraser River sockeye runs far above their low point and there is hope for further expansion of pink stocks. Indeed, we look in vain for any other comparable success in physical rehabilitation of a salmon resource on the Pacific Coast, or for any other investment of $2 million in fishery enhancement with an equivalent return.

The structure of the Commission is simple, and has remained virtually unchanged since its inception. It consists of six members, three from the United States and three from Canada. All are appointed by the federal governments of the two countries. It has been the practice to include representatives of the Province of British Columbia and the state of Washington on the Commission at all times. No action by the Commission is effective unless voted for by at least two commissioners from each country. All expenses incurred by the Commission and its professional staff are shared equally by Canada and the United States.

In an examination of the regulatory process as it is carried on by the International Pacific Salmon Fisheries Commission, two elements deserve special emphasis: the difficulty of obtaining meaningful data, in view of tremendous variance around mean values of expected runs, coupled with limited information and a very short time period in which to harvest the fish; and the increasing complexity of the regulatory opportunities opened up by growing ability to identify separate races and thus the need to treat each, at least to some extent, as a separate management unit.

The preliminary estimates of runs, escapement, and permitted catches are formulated by the Commission each year and form the basis for initial regulations. These are discussed at public hearings and formalized prior to the time when the industry must gear up for the season's fishery. In general, the Commission has attempted to insure a certain percentage escapement, though in recent years increasing knowledge of the sub-groups within the major Fraser River runs has made it possible to estimate absolute numbers of spawners that will approach optimal levels.

As the fishery develops each season, information received daily from the industry and sampling data gathered during days when the commercial fishery is closed enable the Commission staff to formulate an increasingly clear picture of the size, timing, and racial composition of the run. The major regulatory tool employed intra-seasonally is the time closure. Each week the Commission announces open periods by regulatory areas for each of the three major types of gear. This pattern of closure—generally, four to five days per week—may be modified on a short-run basis for two reasons: to adjust for unexpected changes in the size or timing of runs; and to equalize catches by Canadian and American vessels.

The techniques outlined above would present few operating problems if the Fraser River runs followed a regular pattern with respect to timing of movement and if the run could be forecast with reasonable accuracy. In practice, the regulatory authority is plagued by a number of variables that can be quantified only as the fishery develops; and, since the entire operation lasts for only a few weeks, the burden of adjustment becomes extreme. Not only is there wide variation in the time at which the Fraser River fish first arrive in the fishing area, but the rate of movement through the fishery, and therefore the exposure to different types of gear and fishing intensities, shows wide variations, depending on a variety of water and weather conditions. Also, unfavorable water flow conditions in the Fraser may result in "blow-back" of fish; fish may move back into areas open to fishing after entering closed waters as part of the calculated escapement. Fish are extremely vulnerable at this time and may also suffer moderate to serious deterioration in quality if they are held up at the mouth of the river for any prolonged period.

An additional complication is introduced by the variability of migration routes. In 1958, for example, an unusually high proportion of the Fraser River sockeye run came through Johnstone Straits, on the east side of Vancouver Island, which virtually excluded any participation by American fishermen. This would not be of overwhelming concern except for the requirement that the Commission balance the Canadian and American catch of each regulated species from the treaty area *in each year*. Moreover, when the fish come down the east side of Vancouver Island from the north they can be taken in areas outside the regulatory authority of the treaty.

The complexity of the management program of the International Pacific Salmon Fisheries Commission has been increased even further by its research findings. Specifically, substantial improvement in the ability to delineate races of sockeye salmon going to various spawning areas and techniques for identifying each as they appear in the commercial catch make it possible to treat each sub-group separately, to some extent, for management purposes. The significance of such developments is obvious from the discussion in the latter part of Chapter 2. In a complex salmon run, such as that of the Fraser River, in which many separate groups are intermingled, it is highly unlikely that effort directed at each group will be such as to produce optimal escapement, though in average terms approximately the desired escapement appears to be achieved. It is quite possible, particularly with a large and efficient fleet, to harvest nearly 100 percent of particular groups while leaving others virtually untouched. The result is, of course, a significantly lower ratio of returnees to spawners than could be achieved if each race could be managed individually.

This problem would be serious enough under any circumstances, given the variability of the timing of runs and of migration routes and the cost of sampling. It becomes immensely more difficult, however, as a result of the inevitable excess capacity generated in a controlled fishery where the end product is of high value and the potential cost of harvesting relatively low. As indicated above, the Puget Sound fishery has undergone an extraordinary expansion in fishing capacity relative to permitted physical output and, as a result, it has been necessary to restrict fishing time to an average of two to three days per week in recent years. Since both sockeye and pink salmon move through the Puget Sound fishery at considerable speed, the possibility of unbalanced harvesting becomes almost a certainty. During the five

145

closed days, the major part of individual runs may easily escape both Canadian and American fleets, particularly early in the season when the sub-groups tend to move more rapidly. During the two open days, a fleet of some 900 vessels is perfectly capable of catching almost all returning fish from some of the sub-groups. In addition, the very short fishing period restricts severely the flow of information to the Commission staff.

The implications of the requirement that the Commission frame its recommendations to balance the Canadian and American catch are less obvious than they might appear. On the face of it, the requirement virtually dooms the Commission to a series of second-best solutions, year by year, since only the most miraculous of coincidences could assure that closures to balance the catch would also result in optimum escapement. On the other hand, the mere fact that the Canadian and American industries—despite the widely varying shares of the Fraser River run taken by each in past years—were able to agree on any division at all was a notable achievement. It is doubtful that any ratio other than 50-50 would have had any chance of acceptance. While it has no scientific significance, it has a ring of fairness about it that played no small part in the eventual rapprochement. The time may come when the state of our knowledge, the stature of the Commission and its staff, and the obvious advantages to be gained thereby, may permit acceptance of the idea of managing for optimal escapement, with trade-offs over a period of years to even out Canadian-American benefits from the fishery. At the moment, this simply involves more pressure than the still fragile regulatory structure could be expected to stand.

This section has been concerned primarily with the red and pink salmon under the jurisdiction of the Commission. It should be noted that other species of salmon entering the Puget Sound fishery are also subject to detailed management programs, both regulatory and enhancement, carried on by the state of Washington and the national government of Canada. To a limited extent, these policies are coordinated through an interstate compact, the Pacific Marine Fisheries Commission.

CHAPTER 9

Performance of the Puget Sound Fishery: The Economics of Scientific Regulation

〜〜〜〜〜〜〜〜〜〜〜〜〜〜〜〜〜〜〜〜

The analysis of the preceding chapters suggests that the structure of the Puget Sound salmon industry makes it a prime candidate for troublesome economic performance. It is a complex, multispecies fishery, shared by the nationals of two countries, and harvesting high-valued fish that can be caught in close proximity to processing and marketing centers in both Washington and British Columbia. It presents, therefore, a most interesting test of the economic performance of a fishery under "scientific regulation," in a physical sense, with a solid biological research base and substantial regulatory authority.

We have now had almost two decades of experience under such management, with generally close cooperation among fishery authorities and fishing fleets of the two countries involved. Enforcement has been uniformly good, and the Commission itself has been forthright in its resistance to public pressures. In effect, then, we are measuring the economic performance of a well-managed salmon fishery. If those results are unsatisfactory, and if no perceptible self-corrective tendencies can be observed, the strongest possible argument is offered for a shift to a different

THE PACIFIC SALMON FISHERIES

concept of regulation, with economic objectives specified and enhancement of net economic yield an important, though not the sole, criterion by which performance is to be judged.

The general conclusions of the analysis to be developed are as follows:

(1) Conservative estimates suggest that even if no improvements in fishing gear were permitted, all runs of the last 20 years in Puget Sound could have been harvested with two-thirds the amount of gear currently in use. If the number of units of gear were reduced by half, full harvesting would be possible except in the case of one or two exceptionally large runs, and these could have been harvested by the licensing of additional vessels from other areas.

(2) Limited surveys of net earnings of vessel owners and fishermen suggest that returns to capital and labor inputs for all major types of gear have been severely depressed, despite the recovery in runs of the major sockeye species, and despite record prices for most species of salmon. If the number of units had been reduced by as little as one-third, $700,000 to $2.5 million more annually would have been available for additional factor payments and to cover costs of research, development, and management programs.

(3) Physical yields could be increased significantly, but by an unknown amount, if reduction in the number of units of gear permitted spreading intra-seasonal fishing activities of the fleet more evenly. With the amount of gear now in use, the necessity of restricting fishing time to two or three days per week results in severely unbalanced harvesting of the several sub-species that make up the runs to Puget Sound rivers and the Fraser River system. Moreover, the concentration of excess fishing capacity in the two- or three-day fishing period increases enormously the risks of management mistakes. It is quite possible, on the basis of the necessarily fragmentary information that can be developed in two or three fishing days, that individual runs might be almost totally harvested despite what appears to be adequate escapement on an overall basis.

In brief, the economic reaction of the industry to the types of regulation employed has negated most of the potential economic gains from what is otherwise a scientifically sound estimate of aggregate yield potentials and a reasonably effective management program to implement the resulting recommendations. Quite apart from the rash of deliberate efficiency-reducing measures that have plagued the Puget Sound fishery, even flexible and skillful use of time closures results in severe inefficiency in that far more units of gear are in use than are actually required. The economic waste involved is compounded by the fact that the split fishing week does not permit labor to find other employment during the non-fishing periods, since additional fishing time may be allowed at any time on an *ad hoc* basis, and therefore each vessel must be ready to move on very short notice. The inherent tendency toward excess capacity in the fishery has been accentuated by the competitive situation in the canning sector that is even more unstable than in Alaska. As a result, cannery financing of new boats and bonus payments to owners of existing gear have added far more fishing gear to a fleet already larger than is warranted by the availability of fish (or the most optimistic views of future supplies).

Physical Effects of Regulation

A full assessment of physical effects of the Puget Sound regulatory program is beyond the scope of this study. Controversy is still raging over the relative importance of a host of factors that influence the abundance of salmon: fishing intensity, types of fishing gear used, siltation of rivers as a result of poor logging and farming practices, pollution from municipal and industrial abuse of river waters, loss of spawning streams, and a variety of others. We can only present the basic data on trends in landings, with no definitive delineation of the *net* effect of the regulatory program.

The trends in physical landings of Puget Sound salmon since 1913 are shown in Figures 13 through 15. It will be noted that sockeye landings rose perceptibly after the initiation of regulation by the International Pacific Salmon Fisheries Commission in 1946, dropped off after 1958, and recovered again after 1964. Chinook salmon landings, though much smaller than those of other species, have also moved upward very slightly during the

Thousand fish caught

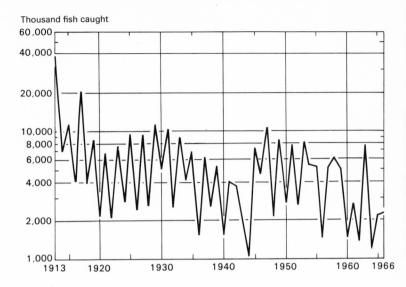

Fig. 13. Puget Sound: Total salmon catch, 1913–66. Source: Table A–7.

Thousand fish caught

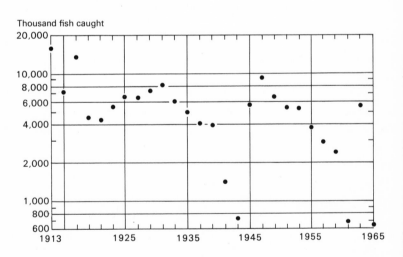

Fig. 14. Puget Sound: Catch of pink salmon in odd-numbered (high) years, 1913–65. Source: Table A–7.

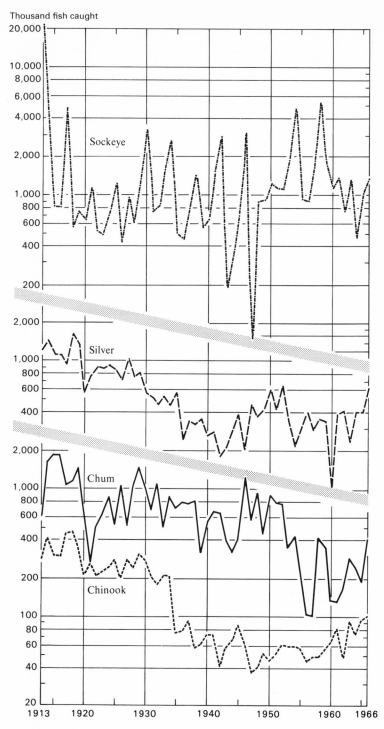

Thousand fish caught

Sockeye

Silver

Chum

Chinook

Fig. 15. Puget Sound: Catch by species of sockeye, chum, silver, and chinook, 1913–66. Source: Table A–7.

past 20 years. The catch of silver salmon has held fairly steady, while landings of both pinks and chums have declined irregularly but persistently since the late 1940's.

Unfortunately, it is quite impossible to decompose these series to give any clear indication of the precise role played by regulation, or, for that matter, to portray accurately the condition of the major stocks involved. For example, the catch of silver salmon appears to have been stabilized, albeit at levels well below the peaks reached in earlier decades, despite the fact that it is subject to a virtually unregulated troll fishery in the ocean and is not under Commission control. The stable catch in recent years probably reflects the conflicting negative effects of increased competition for silvers between Canadian and American trollers and between commercial and sport fishermen on the one hand, and the positive effects of fairly substantial state programs of artificial enhancement and environment improvement on the other.

It is still too early to assess the effect of Commission control over pink salmon; since the program became effective, only a few cycles have elapsed. It is expected that a considerable degree of rehabilitation in the pink salmon runs is possible. Again, this reflects mixed influences, with declines in runs in some Puget Sound rivers more than offset by the long-term prospects for increased catches from the Fraser River run of pinks. Chum salmon have shown a fairly continual decline throughout the Northwest, despite persistent efforts to curtail fishing effort on this particular species. Apparently the reasons for the decline are complex, involving environmental changes as well as excessive fishing effort, and the relatively smaller economic importance of the species has operated to restrict research into the causes of the deterioration in chum stocks.

If we look at Puget Sound salmon landings over a longer period of time, a somewhat different perspective is indicated. Clearly, landings are well below peak levels achieved in previous periods, and it seems unlikely that any economically feasible program regulating fishing effort can restore fully the losses attributable to growth in population, industry, and other elements of human activity that impinge on successful propagation of salmon. Perhaps the best that can be said is that regulation, even before the initiation of more solidly based scientific programs in the late 1940's, has averted a disastrous collapse in landings, and has permitted some recovery in several important areas, notably the Fraser River sockeye.

A full analysis of the impact of the commercial fishery and regulation on the yield of salmon must take into account not only the Puget Sound commercial net fishery but also the effects of the sport fishery, particularly with respect to the silver and chinook catch. As indicated in Figure 16, the sport catch of both species in Puget Sound increased rapidly until 1957. Thereafter, a sharp drop in numbers of fish occurred, reflecting a change in

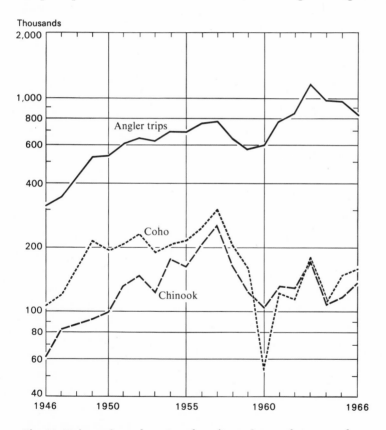

Fig. 16. Estimated number of angler trips and annual sport catch of chinook and coho salmon, Puget Sound and Straits only, 1946–66. Source: Table A–8.

153

regulations which prohibited retention of small salmon previously taken in large numbers by winter and spring fishermen in Puget Sound. Even this is only part of the story. In the past ten years there has been a spectacular increase in the intensity and success of sport fishing effort directed at silvers and chinook salmon off the Washington coast and the mouth of the Columbia River. A substantial proportion of these fish are probably Columbia River fish, but many of them, doubtless, are of Puget Sound origin.

It should also be noted that the apparent slight increase in chinook landings in the Puget Sound net fishery conceals a decline of alarming proportions in the overall coastwide catch of chinooks. Again, this reflects in part the influence of continued rapid growth in the outside troll fishery carried on by both Canadian and American fishermen—a fishery that is regulated only to a very slight degree by seasonal closure and minimum size limits.

On balance, it would appear that increases in the catch of some species are as yet insufficient to offset a persistent decline in others. Although it is carried out in one of the intensely regulated fisheries in the world, the overall program cannot be counted a full success even in a physical sense. The single factor of overwhelming importance in the recovery of the Fraser River sockeye runs was a once-for-all correction of the blockage at Hell's Gate. It should also be noted that the commercial landings in Puget Sound have been supplemented by a hatchery and natural rearing program of moderate proportions. While data are as yet too fragmentary to permit accurate estimates of the contribution of the hatcheries to the commercial catch, a recent study of the contribution of the natural rearing ponds suggests that the benefits received were only a small fraction of the total costs incurred.[1] In short, it seems that the Puget Sound stocks remain in precarious condition despite the level and complexity of the regulatory measures employed.

[1] J. A. Crutchfield, Kenneth Kral, and Lloyd Phinney, *An Economic Evaluation of Washington State Department of Fisheries' Controlled Natural-Rearing Program for Coho Salmon*, State of Washington Department of Fisheries, August 1965.

Trends in Fishing Effort

Much more disturbing evidence of the long-range impact of regulation on the Puget Sound fishery is found in the amounts of gear employed and the catch per unit of effort. Figures 17 and 18 indicate the extent of the increase in fishing licenses issued since 1935 for the three principal types of salmon gear and the decline in catch per unit of gear. Even when we allow for the tendency in recent years to license a considerable number of

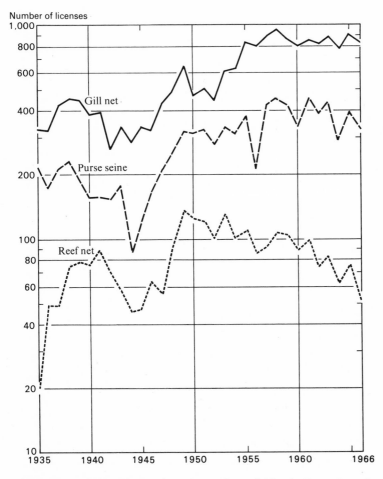

Number of licenses

Fig. 17. Number of licenses issued for salmon fishing in Puget Sound, 1935–66. Source: Table A–9.

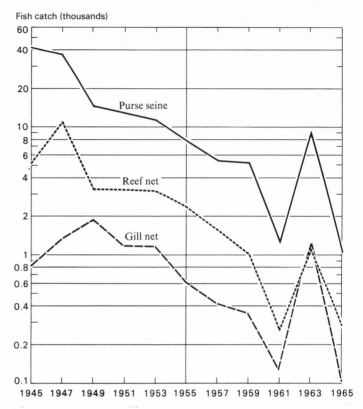

Fish catch (thousands)

Fig. 18. Puget Sound: Average pink salmon catch per license issued, in odd-numbered (high) years, 1945–65. Source: Tables A–7 and A–9.

boats not actually used for fishing, it is obvious that a major increase in capital and labor inputs occurred during a period when the general trend in landings was stable or downward.

Unfortunately, it is difficult to link the figures for catch per unit effort for earlier years with those for the years in which regulations assumed their present status. As indicated in Chapter 8, elimination of the traps in 1935 resulted in a statistical gap that is impossible to rectify, since it was several years before operators of the remaining types of gear were able to discover and develop the most profitable areas of fishing activity given

156

the removal of the traps and associated restrictions.[2] As in the Alaskan case, it is impossible to account statistically for the progressively more severe restrictions on technical innovation that have been introduced over the years as a means of coping with the expanded fishing capacity of the enlarged fleet. But the figures, even as they stand, demonstrate that even a closely and scientifically regulated fishery, if subject to completely unrestricted entry, will produce persistent factor malallocation, the severity of which is functionally related to real prices for end products as compared to real costs of fishing effort.

Prices to fishermen for Puget Sound salmon increased substantially during the period 1935–66. It is hardly surprising, then, that the increase in fishing units was as large as it was, or that efforts to restrict improvements in the efficiency of individual units of gear were so strenuous and effective.

Another factor accounting for the tremendous growth in licensed gear is the unstable equilibrium in the processing industry, discussed in Chapter 8. Excess capacity has been almost chronic in the processing sector for 20 to 30 years, and the desperate struggle to obtain sufficient fish to keep unit costs within reason has been a major factor in boosting the number of fishing units in the Puget Sound area.

The 1963 study of the Puget Sound fishery indicated that various types of bonus payments accounted for as much as 12 to 15 percent of the total gross receipts of fishing vessels.[3] Experience of British Columbia packers parallels that of the Puget Sound area.[4] In effect, the entire economic rent from the fishery (and at least some part of the quasi-rent accruing to capital equipment in the canning sector) has been transferred to the

[2] This is not mere conjecture. It was pointed out to us by Dr. Milo Bell, former Director of Fisheries for the state, who mounted a determined, but basically unsuccessful, effort to establish the linkage.

[3] W. Royce, D. Bevan, J. Crutchfield, G. Paulik, and R. Fletcher, *Salmon Gear Limitation in Northern Washington Waters,* University of Washington Publications in Fisheries, New Series, Vol. II, No. 1, 1963.

[4] See S. Sinclair, *License Limitation—British Columbia: A Method of Economic Fisheries Management* (Department of Fisheries of Canada, Ottawa, 1960).

labor input in the fisheries in order to maintain existing catch levels.[5] This has not accrued as increases in real incomes to individual fishermen and vessel owners, however; it has simply increased the number of underemployed vessels and men.

INCOMES IN THE PUGET SOUND FISHERY

The general economic situation of the Washington-based portion of the Puget Sound fishery can be outlined from data obtained in the 1963 study for the years 1959–61. The average purse seiner, for example, showed annual gross receipts of $36,600, of which $4,600 represented "incentive payments" from buyers. Total net returns to the owners of the vessels, including their own shares as working fishermen, averaged $8,200. If owners' shares are deducted as part of actual labor costs—the proper treatment—profits averaged approximately $5,000. There is fairly wide dispersion around these mean figures based on the individual skill of fishermen.

These figures overstate the actual net return to vessel owners by a substantial margin, however. Most of the equipment employed has been fully depreciated for tax purposes, and many of the hulls are being depreciated on a basis that bears no relationship to present construction costs. Three Puget Sound boatyards estimated the replacement cost of the hull, motor, and equipment of a purse seiner of the same size and type as those surveyed at about $77,000 including the value of the skiff used in purse seining. Using the same depreciation rates as those now employed for tax purposes, net income to the owner of a new vessel would be about $3,100, a return of only 3.9 percent. It should also be noted that maintenance costs for these vessels are badly understated in accounting records, since much repair and maintenance work is performed by the owners. If the costs of these services were imputed at current wage rates, the rate of return realized during the years in question would almost certainly be negative for the group surveyed, though the wide

[5] This is consistent with Rubinstein's findings about industry profits and his rationale for the current wave of consolidations in the processing sector. M. E. Rubinstein, "The History of Concentration in the Canned Salmon Industry of the United States" (unpublished Bachelor's thesis, Harvard University, 1966), Appendix A.

variances characteristic of fishing incomes would show some fairly attractive returns for a few individual boats each year.

Finally, it is evident that returns from fish catches alone would have left these vessels in a loss position during the entire period in question. Only the hidden "incentive payments," which did not go through the share mechanism, enabled the boats to cover contractual operating costs. It might be noted, parenthetically, that only a few vessel owners were required to pay interest on indebtedness to canners and that costs of fuel, food, and supplies were frequently understated because the fish purchaser paid the bills. There was no practical way to estimate the extent of the resulting understatement of costs, but it was substantial.

Income data for gill netters and reef netters are almost impossible to obtain from conventional survey techniques except at prohibitive cost. The casual nature of the Puget Sound gill net fishery, with its emphasis on part-time operation, is indicated by the following figures. More than a quarter of the 600 gill netters surveyed obtained some income from other salmon fishing; and more than 54 percent engaged in non-fishing occupations during the years in question. Unemployment compensation was paid to 17 percent of the gill netters in 1959, and to 25 percent in 1961.

On these grounds, it is obvious that really meaningful figures could not be obtained for income from all sources. Unreliable as they are, however, the figures derived from the 1963 survey are the only data available for gill netters. The data indicate an average gross income for these operators from Puget Sound fishing of $2,300 for the odd years 1959–61, and in 1960, when no pink salmon were available, only $1,700. On the basis of very rough estimates of cost, net returns averaged less than half these amounts. It is not surprising that gill-netting is almost entirely a part-time operation, and that fishermen are heavily dependent on non-fishing income even during the best years. The average investment in a gill net vessel ranged from $6,000 to $7,000 during the period in question, and the current replacement cost of a modern gill netter would vary from $11,000 to $15,000. It is likely that if account were taken of all imputed costs for labor performed by the owner, the return on capital in the gill net operation ranges from zero to negative values most of the time.

If it were not for the substantial assistance of the canners in the form of bonus payments, it is highly unlikely that the gill net fleet, outdated and inefficient as it is, would even be maintained.

For a variety of reasons, insufficient data were received from reef netters to permit any evaluation of their economic status in the survey years. Part of the reluctance of the reef netters to provide this information stems from the fact that their trade association, which includes all active reef net operators, has developed a kind of *de facto* property right for each reef net location licensed by the state of Washington. Over a period of some ten years, the number of reef nets actually fished has been reduced substantially, with the expected result: the economic position of the reef netters appears to be more satisfactory than that of any other type of gear. This is true, of course, only as long as owners of other types of gear are not permitted to fish in the reef net locations. Nevertheless, it indicates clearly the direct relationship between unrestricted entry and the marginal or submarginal economic position of Puget Sound fishermen in most other operations.

A mail questionnaire was used to obtain income data from employed fishermen in the Puget Sound purse seine fleet. Unfortunately, the response with respect to income from sources other than salmon fishing was very limited. It was possible, however, to obtain usable figures on earnings from the Puget Sound salmon operation. The average share received averaged about $1,100 per man-year from 1959 through 1961. This is consistent with the figures derived for share payments by purse seine vessel owners, which averaged about $1,900 but included some income from fishing in Alaska. It is not surprising that respondents drew unemployment compensation in 59 percent of the man-years reported in the survey. The fishery not only yields an unsatisfactory level of incomes for labor inputs, but involves substantial transfer payments from other state residents who contribute to the unemployment insurance program.

POTENTIAL ECONOMIC RENT

It is impossible to find a base period, comparable to that used in the analysis of Chapter 7, from which potential net economic yield could be estimated. The 1963 study does, however, provide an acceptable alternative approach, based on a computer simulation of the Puget Sound runs coupled with physical efficiency and area utilization studies for the three major types of net fishing gear. The biometric model permits us to estimate the effects on landings and permitted fishing days of any alteration in the amounts of gear employed on various assumptions as to the amount of escapement desired by the regulatory authority. With price and cost data developed by direct analysis of accounting statements, it is possible to approximate the rents that would be available with alternative reductions in gear.

Costs of operation for the three types of gear were broken down into three categories: (1) labor costs (including fishing shares to owners), which vary directly with value of the catch of the individual boat; (2) running costs, which vary directly with fishing time and include fuel, groceries, and part of repairs and supplies; and (3) fixed costs, which are committed for the season and are independent of the number of days the vessel actually fishes. This category would include investment and gearing costs such as depreciation, insurance, licenses, moorage, property taxes, and a portion of repairs and supplies.

If we now assume a reduction of one-third or one-half in the number of units of gear of all types, ignoring for the moment the method of accomplishing this, the following reactions on costs may be expected. Total running costs for the fleet would remain essentially the same, since running time for a larger number of vessels will simply be reallocated to a smaller number fishing a greater number of days. Gearing and investment costs would be reduced proportionately, since these are a function of the number of vessels employed. Labor costs would also be reduced proportionately, though this is not immediately apparent. The basic result of lengthening the fishing week through reduction in the number of units fishing would be to release a proportionate number of fishermen to other occupations. Those remaining in the fishery would work a greater number of days, but under present arrangements intra-seasonal closed periods are normally too short and too irregular to permit fishermen to engage in significant amounts of other work during the fishing season. Consequently, the increased number of days actually devoted to fishing by men on the remaining vessels would involve little or no loss of production elsewhere in the economy.

The results of these calculations for representative years are indicated in Table 7. It is apparent that the savings realized are

Table 7. *Potential Savings from 50 Percent Gear Reduction, Selected Years*
(thousand dollars)

Gear	1955	1956	1958	1959
Purse seine	1,950	553	2,822	670
Gill net	462	573	814	294
Reef net	227	150	135	88
Total reduction in cost	2,639	1,276	3,771	1,052

Source: *Salmon Gear Limitation in Northern Washington Waters*, Royce, Bevan, Crutchfield, Paulik, Fletcher, University of Washington Publications in Fisheries, New Series, Vol. II, No. 1, 1963.

far from trivial even under the extremely conservative assumptions underlying the preceding calculations. Regardless of the final disposition of the increased net economic yield made available through an effective gear reduction program, a significant improvement in the economic position of all participants can be realized, together with increased license fees to cover at least some of the costs of management now charged to general revenues.

IMPROVED TECHNOLOGY AND POTENTIAL RENT

It is impossible to estimate with any degree of accuracy the additional savings that could be realized if the restrictive assumptions underlying these calculations were relaxed. For a variety of reasons, it was considered essential at the time of the 1963 study to assume proportional reductions in all types of gear employed. It is quite obvious, however, from the computer simulation program that changes in the number of units of gear fishing and in the number of days of fishing permitted during the open season would produce significantly different effects on the physical productivity of different types of gear. Thus, if the gear reduction program were extended to permit shifts in the composition of different types of gear on the basis of economic efficiency, the aggregate cost of any given catch could be further reduced.

There are, moreover, a variety of other external diseconomies that could be reduced or eliminated once the overwhelming threat of grossly excessive capacity is alleviated. The following are most significant:

(1) All types of gear used in Puget Sound, particularly the purse seiners, run into diminishing returns in the Marshallian sense as a result of congestion on the better fishing grounds. Interference and competition among the individual boats in a given fishing area are major factors reducing the efficiency of each unit in the Puget Sound salmon fishery.

(2) As indicated in Chapter 2, the regulatory program in Puget Sound (and in Alaska and British Columbia as well) includes many restrictions designed to prevent adoption of more efficient gear. Once the principle of gear limitation is accepted and its beneficial results demonstrated, it should be possible to relax restrictions on gear efficiency now required to keep the management program within bounds. On the basis of perfectly feasible productivity studies, the number of units of gear that would have to be withdrawn with each increase in the efficiency of any type of equipment could be calculated and worked into the longer-range program of reduction in factor inputs. For example, relaxation of restrictions on the use of monofilament nylon gill nets, the length and depth of both gill nets and seines, and electronic fish finding equipment could increase the productivity of the individual unit immediately.

(3) The quality of the end product could be improved if deliveries to packers were spread over a four- or five-day week. At present, fish must be held under refrigeration in order to operate the cannery on a full weekly schedule, and current technology makes it impossible to hold fish for more than a day or two in chilled brine. In most cases, quality does not suffer, but only because additional expenses are incurred for storage under refrigeration.

(4) Concentration of landings in two or three days per week during the fishing season increases greatly the loss from breakdown for the individual vessel. At present, a breakdown during

the peak of the season, even if it means only the loss of a day or two of fishing, can cut the gross income of a fishing vessel in Puget Sound by as much as 20 or 25 percent.

(5) Extension of the fishing week to four or five days would permit far more efficient use of the regulatory powers of the Commission. The longer the fishing week, the greater the range and accuracy of information reaching the Commission and the more precise its regulatory actions. In addition, the dangerously large number of units now fishing raises the possibility of unavoidable errors that could do serious damage to sub-sections of the Fraser River populations. It will be recalled from Chapter 2 that the life cycle of the salmon guarantees a very long time lag between excessive fishing, recognition of that fact, and effective remedial action.

(6) A final modification of the findings above with respect to potential increases in net economic yield under a program of restricted entry involves the selectivity process inherent in the method of reduction chosen. It seems likely, on *a priori* grounds, that almost any program of gear reduction that permits voluntary sale and retirement of licenses and gear (and that ultimately aims at conversion of licenses into transferable property rights) will operate to concentrate gear and licenses in the hands of more skillful and more productive fishermen. A study of the British Columbia salmon fishery, for example, indicated that as much as 50 percent of the gear presently licensed could be removed before any really appreciable reduction in effective fishing capacity would be achieved. While this was offered as an argument against gear limitation, it would appear to us to be a very strong argument in favor of it.

Some biologists and management authorities have expressed grave concern about the ability of the fleet to harvest unusually large runs if a really effective gear limitation program were undertaken. This reflects in part the confusion over biological and economic concepts of waste, but it also involves an allegedly significant problem of reduced productivity from excessive numbers of fish on the spawning grounds. The argument seems more apparent than real. In the first place, the fish seemed to flourish in the period prior to any fishing, so the effects of "excessive escape-

164

ment" would not be too serious. Second, excessive escapement would only be a problem in the case of an unexpectedly large run. If the run were forecast with a reasonable degree of accuracy, it would be easy enough to make arrangements to license additional vessels, and there would be an incentive to use these licenses. Even where an unexpectedly large run does develop, the fact will become apparent early enough to permit additional vessels to enter the fishery if required. Moreover, if a 50 percent reduction in gear would generally allow only a four- or five-day fishing week, adding additional fishing days up to the limit of seven and extending fishing hours would permit a very substantial increase in effective capacity of a given fleet.

We conclude that the possibility of economic loss from inability to harvest fully or from excessive escapement from spawning grounds is far outweighed by the saving that could be realized by even moderate reductions in the number of fishing units. Quite apart from the flexibility argument above, it would be perfectly feasible to divert unnecessary spawners from the grounds in the event of unexpectedly large escapement and still incur far lower costs over time than would be required to maintain "stand-by capacity" sufficient to harvest even the largest runs. This was done at the Adams River in 1958 because the industry was saturated with fish.

The unstable competitive situation that leads packers to finance an excessive number of vessels might also lead them for the same reasons to pay excessive prices for restricted numbers of licenses. There are probably good grounds for arguing that a restricted entry situation would leave the packer with less incentive than he now feels to engage in this self-defeating process. Even if there were a tendency for packers to integrate backward into direct operation of fishing vessels, however, it is not certain that the economic results would be entirely undesirable. From the standpoint of fisheries management, it may be that integration of fishing and processing operations would improve both the accuracy and the efficiency of the regulatory program. In addition, the increase in fishermen's incomes that would inevitably follow a program of gear reduction, to the extent that it permits independent financing of vessels and gear, might well produce at least a segment of the fishing fleet capable of maintaining a truly independent status—something that is nearly impossible under present conditions, since the very existence of the purse seine fleet and most of the gill net fleet is dependent on continued bonus payments by canners.

In these circumstances, it seems clear that the estimate of potential net economic yield in the original University of Washington study is extremely conservative, since it ignores entirely the possible savings mentioned above. If we assume, not illogically, that the value of Puget Sound salmon landings to Washington fishermen will average in the neighborhood of $10 million to $12 million annually, a gear reduction program that permits a four- or five-day fishing week and the elimination of some of the more onerous restrictions on efficient gear could result in a flow of annual net benefits of $5 million to $7 million. This would provide opportunity incomes for all participants, even after diversion of sufficient funds, through taxes and license fees, to cover the allocable costs of research, development, and management incurred by the state and the Commission. The implications of benefit-cost analysis of research and development expenditures by federal and state agencies concerned with salmon are discussed in the following chapter. At this point we merely note that the actual net economic yield from the Puget Sound salmon fishery becomes negative if one allocates to it any reasonable part of current research and management costs.

In effect, then, it is argued that a rational management program in the Puget Sound salmon fishery would provide a viable industry, capable of making a sizable net economic contribution to regional and national economies. This is in sharp contrast to the present situation, which clearly results in a negative contribution to net national product, despite the substantial market value of the high-valued species that make up the bulk of the catch. As in the Alaska case, this is a discouraging conclusion, since it suggests that 40 years of developing technical and managerial skill in the salmon program and a skillful, research-oriented program, in operation since 1946, have brought little or nothing in the way of net economic gains. The potential is there; but in the absence of any attention to economic criteria of performance or of the economic reactions of the fishery to the regulations themselves, the conclusion seems inescapable that in Puget Sound, as elsewhere, we have completely failed to capitalize on the opportunity presented by the fishery scientist.

In assessing the success of the salmon management program of the International Pacific Salmon Fisheries Commission, one must be careful to distinguish elements of weakness inherent in the setting of the program from those that reflect inadequate organization, concept, or performance. The preceding discussion has stressed the inadequacies in concept—specifically the proscription of any power to limit entry—that have led to serious economic waste. It should also be recognized, however, that the Commission has functioned with a high degree of skill and firmness in dealing with difficult managerial problems.

As has been stressed in many other connections, all public policy decisions involve lags in perception, formulation of decision, and effect of action. In the case of the Puget Sound salmon fishery, all three are highly significant. Even if the fishery were so managed as to permit five or six days of operation each week during the season, there is a considerable lag from the beginning of the run to the time at which the Commission can make a reasonably accurate assessment of its size and racial composition. The decision-making process can be and is rapid and those decisions are translated into action with a minimum of delay— usually no more than a day. Even so, with the tremendous excess capacity now actively employed in or available to the fishery, a great deal of unintended exploitation can take place even in a one-day period. The situation is, of course, accentuated severely by the progressive shortening of the intra-seasonal fishing period that has been required as a result of unimpeded entry.

A far more serious limitation on precise management of the Puget Sound salmon resources is inherent in the biology of the organism. The long-run efforts of any given regulatory action can be assessed, even if all else remains unchanged, only after two or three life cycles have been completed. In the simplest terms, this means that only major actions by the Commission can be evaluated after one or two cycles; the results of less important actions and the more subtle effects can hardly be detected except over much longer periods. Moreover, as the discussion of Chapter 2 makes clear, the assumption that all else remains unchanged is more than suspect.

To disentangle the efforts of a management decision from the effects of the myriad factors in nature operating over the same time period to alter the size and composition of the stock is a heroic task. Obviously, the Commission's technical staff is well aware of the significance of the tremendous variance around mean values of the functions relating fishing effort to yield. There can be little doubt that it has narrowed the boundaries of our ignorance about the physical parameters that determine the annual yield available from the Puget Sound salmon resource. But the fact remains that any management program must contain sufficient slack to permit the Commission to act quickly and decisively to meet unexpected developments.

In brief, the economics of salmon management in Puget Sound must always be an exercise in second best, and any attempt to charge the Commission with adherence to a simple maximizing model runs the risk of potentially severe damage from time to time. Salmon management must remain an art to some extent. This is not to deny the primacy of the economic definition of the objectives of management; it is simply a plea for recognition of the large area that must remain within human discretion.

CHAPTER 10

An Alternative Regulatory Program

The analysis to this point suggests a number of reasons for dissatisfaction with present concepts of fishery management in general and salmon management in particular. Before launching a discussion of our own proposals, let us examine briefly the relation of our case study areas to the total salmon catch of the Pacific Coast and to attempt at least a rough estimate of the total rent available. The effect of high-seas salmon fishing by the Japanese (and, potentially, by others) on the Pacific Coast catch must also be considered. Unless the gains are worthwhile—and appear to be attainable throughout a wide range of the world's fisheries—there is no point in undertaking the very real political effort required to implement a radically new concept of regulation.

TOTAL POTENTIAL NET ECONOMIC YIELD

In Chapters 7 and 9, we indicated two alternative methods of calculating the economic rent now dissipated in the Bristol Bay and Puget Sound fisheries. The first indicated the amount of rent that might be realized in Bristol Bay using the best technology available in a previous base period with the minimum number of units required, modified by a rough estimate of the productivity effects of technological change that occurred between the base period and the present. It is conservative on several grounds, particularly because no further technological change was forecast nor was any allowance made for improved physical yields as a result of a more manageable control program if excess capacity were removed. Unfortunately, no appropriate base period is available that would permit use of this technique in other salmon fisheries.

The Puget Sound estimate is even more conservative, since it was predicated not only on the assumption that restoration of the traps would be politically unfeasible but also that reduction of excess capacity would have to be proportional for all existing types of gear, regardless of shifts in technological efficiency with reduction in fishing pressure that might favor one type of gear over another. As in the Bristol Bay case, no allowance was made for future technological progress or for improvement in managerial efficiency of the control authority with reduced fishing capacity.

Despite the conservatism of these estimates, the total amount of rent that could be realized based on existing prices and the assumptions mentioned above amounted to approximately $3.5 million and $6 million respectively.

There are other fragmentary studies that permit us to estimate roughly the potential yield from several other portions of the Pacific Coast salmon fishery. Fry's excellent study of the Sacramento River[1] which accounts for the major part of all salmon landings in California is based on much the same set of assumptions underlying the Puget Sound computations, except that his task was much simpler. The Sacramento run consists entirely of chinook salmon (steelhead are not fished commercially) and only one type of gear need be considered—a representative gill netter using monofilament nylon nets. Since past records of the commercial gill net fishery on the Sacramento provide excellent data on the timing of the runs, it is possible to simulate fairly accurately the effects of alternative amounts of fishing effort, in total and by individual boat, and thus to determine the fishing capacity (i.e., the minimum number of optimum-sized gill netters)

[1] Donald H. Fry, *Potential Profits in the California Salmon Fishery*, California Fish and Game, published by the Resources Agency of California, Vol. 48, No. 4, October 1962.

required to harvest the permitted catch while yielding desired escapement.

Fry estimates that runs averaging $3.3 million in value to the fishermen could be harvested regularly at an annual cost of approximately $330,000, yielding a potential rent of about $3 million. This does not take into account possible reductions in cost allocable to the salmon operation if the gill netters could be employed in other fisheries during off-season periods. The resulting estimate of net rent seems very large as a proportion of gross revenue, but it must be remembered that the Sacramento could be harvested more easily than almost any other salmon stream on the Pacific Coast, and that salmon entering the Sacramento are all high-valued chinook, in excellent condition for delivery to the major fresh and frozen fish markets centered in the San Francisco Bay area. If it were possible to value the sport catch accurately (Fry simply valued all fish at the current price to commercial fishermen), the figure would doubtless be even higher.

For several reasons we have no comparable estimates of potential net economic yield from the Columbia River system. The most serious obstacle to such calculations is the fact that the wide ranging Columbia River chinook are taken in troll and sport fisheries from northern California to central Alaska, and the large-scale tagging programs necessary to determine accurately the contribution of the Columbia to troll and sport catches over that wide area are not yet complete. In addition, a high proportion of the total catch of the Columbia, like that of the Sacramento, is taken by sport fishermen, and there is no satisfactory method of evaluating the recreation contribution (as distinct from the catch itself). Since they would be worth, as a minimum, the opportunity cost implicit in the price paid to troll fishermen, valuation of the sport catch at commercial prices, the only feasible alternative at present, is excessively conservative.[2] Moreover, the Columbia presents serious complications with respect to simula-

[2] W. G. Brown, E. Castle, and A. Singh, *An Economic Evaluation of the Oregon Salmon and Steelhead Sport Fishery,* Oregon Agricultural Experiment Station Technical Bulletin 78 (Corvallis: Oregon State University, September 1964). Their estimate of total *net* economic yield, which utilizes an analytically sound procedure, is much greater than that derived from the use of commercial prices to value the sport catch.

tion procedures. It supports runs of blueback (sockeye), coho, and steelhead (which can be taken commercially in Oregon), in addition to several distinct races of chinook. The resulting changes in the composition of gill net catches, together with the complex hydrological regime of the lower Columbia River and the erratic behavior of the fish when they first enter the lower stretches of the river, make it much more difficult than on the Sacramento to simulate catches under different assumptions as to types and quantities of gear employed.

The question of the appropriate technology to use in calculating potential net economic rent is also more difficult in the case of the Columbia. If our point of reference is the most efficient presently available technique, the obvious method of harvesting would be at the first high dam for all fish going upstream, with traps or other fixed devices to harvest fish in the lower tributaries of the Columbia rather than in the main river. Alternatively, one could calculate the economic rent that would be realized by an optimal fleet of modern gill netters operating near the mouth of the river.

The latter procedure would present real problems in the Columbia, however, since the runs of fish are mixed at any given period, and variations in the size of fish would require the use of different mesh sizes to harvest various segments of the population in the river at any given time. In addition, gill netters kill some fish which drop out of the nets. A fleet of controlled size would presumably work out an optimal set of compromises, assuming reasonable sampling and information as to the fish available at any given period, but no operating experience exists that would permit approximation of this pattern by simulation. Moreover, it would still be far short of the efficiency that could be realized, with respect to both harvesting and escapement, by taking all upriver fish at the first fish passage facility. Balanced against this, of course, would be some loss of quality as the time of capture moves farther and farther upstream. This is far less serious in the case of the Columbia than in any other salmon river except the Yukon, since the major runs in the Columbia spawn far upstream and remain in marketable condition even when they reach the tributaries in Idaho. Nevertheless, maximum economic yield would doubtless require that at least some fish be harvested by the troll fleet in the open sea and some in the lower river. The optimal division cannot even be guessed at on the basis of present information.

One final complication might be noted. If the analysis is viewed in completely timeless terms, the stream of annual costs reflecting user costs of the heavy capital investment in fish passage and hatchery operations on the Columbia should be charged to the fishery. On the other hand, if the fisheries are viewed only prospectively, some of the expenditures—particularly for fish passage facilities built into the dams themselves—should be regarded as sunk costs, irrelevant for purposes of future valuation of the fishery.

If we assume, realistically, that the present proportion of the total catch of Columbia River chinooks and silvers will be caught at sea by trollers, with the river catch harvested by efficient mobile gear in the lower river, an estimate of potential net economic yield of 75 percent of the gross value to fishermen is conservative.

With an average value for the commercial catch attributable to the Columbia of approximately $6.7 million between 1960 and 1964,[3] this calculation indicates a potential annual net yield of the order of $5 million. To this must be added approximately $4.7 million for the very large ocean and river sport catch of Columbia River chinook and cohoes.[4]

Without consideration of subsequent technological improvements, there is therefore an annual return of nearly $10 million potentially available, to cover research and management costs and for distribution among contributing factors.

No data are available that would permit direct estimates of potential rent from the salmon fishery of British Columbia or from those of any part of Alaska other than Bristol Bay. With respect to British Columbia, however, it is likely that the Puget

[3] These figures have been adjusted to reflect supplementary payments by packers to fishermen above actual ex-vessel prices. For details, see the U.S. Fish and Wildlife study entitled *An Economic Evaluation of the Columbia River Fishery Development Program* (mimeo.).

[4] Based on an extrapolation to the Columbia River catch of the values developed in the definitive study by Brown, Castle, and Singh, *op. cit.*

Sound figures would be reasonably representative. Almost half of British Columbia's catch comes from precisely the same fishery, and there is little reason to feel that the operating results on the other side of the boundary would be significantly different than those of the Washington fleet. The only significant difference in the fleets is that reef nets are not used in the British Columbia operation; but, since they account for only about 3 to 5 percent of the Washington catch, this is not a serious qualification. In addition, much of the remaining British Columbia sockeye catch is taken from the Skeena River system under essentially similar conditions, though it is not under international regulation. Again leaving the sport and troll fisheries out of consideration, the potential net yield, assuming a reduction in gear paralleling that in the Washington fishery, would average about $15 million on the basis of 1960–65 catches and prices.

Much the same comments would apply to southeastern Alaska. Many of the vessels sampled in the Puget Sound survey also fish in that area, and the operating results for similar types of gear are closely comparable. In central and western Alaska, however, fishing conditions vary so widely from area to area that it is difficult to relate the potential net economic yield to that of either Bristol Bay or Puget Sound. A figure of 50 percent of net yield in these areas and in southeast Alaska appears reasonable, and as conservative as the estimates for other areas.

The results of these estimates of the potential net economic yield of the major Pacific Coast commercial salmon fisheries are summarized below:

	million dollars
Alaska	20.5
British Columbia	15.0
Puget Sound (U.S.)	6.0
Columbia River	5.0
Sacramento River	3.0
Total	49.5

It should be reiterated that, while these estimates are only very crude approximations, they are heavily biased on the conservative side and should be regarded as minima. The suggested savings would be realized through changes that would reduce sharply the possibility of serious errors in judgment by regulatory authorities; it would improve the flow of intra-seasonal information to the management agencies; and it would open the long-dormant incentive for further technological development of the fishery. In terms of the regional economies involved, it cannot reasonably be argued that these quantities are trivial. No one should minimize the enormous difficulties of devising politically acceptable programs that would move us in the direction of an efficient fishing and management program, but it can hardly be denied that the stakes are high enough to make the effort worthwhile.

A RECOMMENDED PROGRAM FOR GEAR REDUCTION

Assumptions and Constraints

Any program of regulation for the salmon industry that would produce significant improvement in its economic performance requires that the ground rules be made explicit. The following are most significant. First, it is assumed that the power of the regulatory agency to reduce the number of operating units to some optimal level and to prevent further new entry would meet the test of constitutionality, both state and federal. Fletcher's excellent summary in the Puget Sound study,[5] though carefully qualified, suggests strongly that this is not a major obstacle as far as the salmon fisheries of Washington state are concerned. The essence of Fletcher's argument may be summarized as follows. If a gear reduction program is based on a reasonable consideration of relevant facts by the legislature, if limited access to the fishery is administered without discrimination, and if the objective is to enhance the *general* welfare of state residents, it should meet the several constitutional tests that might be raised. As Fletcher points out, his analysis applies only to the general principle of gear reduction. Any specific program must, of course, be examined very carefully with respect to the legality of its major provisions. Nevertheless, it appears that factually sup-

---

[5] W. Royce, D. Bevan, J. Crutchfield, G. Paulik and R. Fletcher, *Salmon Gear Limitation in Northern Washington Waters*, University of Washington Publications in Fisheries, New Series, Vol. II, No. 1, 1963, pp. 52–117.

ported recommendations for a gear reduction plan could be formulated into legislation that would probably pass judicial scrutiny.

The situation in Alaska is not so clear. The state constitution contains a provision specifically guaranteeing access to the fisheries for all citizens of the state: unquestionably a reaction to what Alaskans regard as serious abuses by absentee owners of traps during the early days of the Alaska fishery. Whether this constitutes a complete prohibition against a program that meets the tests outlined above is uncertain. In any event, there are no immutable legal obstacles to the initiation of a controlled reduction of inputs in the salmon fisheries, though the practical politics of the situation might make it far more difficult to achieve in Alaska than in British Columbia or the Pacific Coast states.

Secondly, it is assumed that both sound economic policy and considerations of equity require that any gear reduction program be framed and timed to minimize individual hardship and compulsion. This implies that the rate of reduction in fishing units should be geared to normal attrition of men and vessels, unless specifically accelerated by a program of voluntary exit through purchase and retirement of fishing rights and gear by a public agency.

Finally, the analysis of Chapter 2 makes it abundantly clear that variations in salmon runs as a result of natural factors are so wide and unpredictable in our present state of knowledge that the optimal level of fishing gear will doubtless be higher than would be the case if we could forecast with precision the exact amount of harvesting capacity required. Although control of the numbers of fishing units would become a primary management weapon, it would still be necessary to use time and area closures as the elements of a flexible defense against unexpected developments. Over time, however, it should be possible to remove the more onerous of the restrictions on gear efficiency.

In these terms, a practical and legally acceptable method of reducing fishing capacity to more sensible levels breaks down into five elements: (1) How should the reduction actually be achieved? (2) How rapidly should this reduction proceed? (3) On what basis should the restricted number of licenses be distributed to individual vessel owners? (4) How should the reduction in gear be distributed among the various types of fishing equipment now in use? (5) Should the economic gains be apportioned among fishermen, processors and distributors, and government through market forces alone, or should government intervene?

Recommended Program: Puget Sound

The following elements of a gear reduction program for the Puget Sound salmon fishery of Washington were formulated on the basis of the 1963 study by the University of Washington group.[6]

(1) The number of units of gear of each type should be frozen temporarily at the level prevailing in the last fishing season. It would appear both feasible and desirable to reduce the number of licenses immediately by weeding out licenses for vessels which have not fished for salmon within the past few years. By eliminating much of the "blank ticket licensing" encouraged by the present system, it would be possible to start with a level of licensed gear which corresponds to the number of vessels actually fishing commercially.[7]

(2) License fees should be raised to levels which bear a more realistic relationship to the value of the fishing privilege conferred. This would eliminate much of the strictly casual commercial fishing and the quasi-commercial fishing of some sportsmen,

---

[6] *Ibid.*, pp. 118–20. It should be noted that some actions have been taken in British Columbia to implement the first two of the steps listed.

As this study was going to press the government of British Columbia announced that it plans to initiate a system of entry controls for salmon fishing in 1969. Licenses will be issued only to those vessels that have taken salmon in the past two years, and they will be issued in two categories—large and small vessels. No new vessels can participate in the fishery unless they replace a vessel in the large-size category. The licenses of vessels that are removed from the fishery by accident or lost at sea will be cancelled and cannot be replaced. It is anticipated that as the fishing privilege becomes more valuable, due to the reduction of the size of the fleet, vessel license fees will be increased. Department of Fisheries, *Fisheries of Canada*, Vol. 21, No. 4 (October 1968).

[7] This refers to the common practice among the canners of licensing vessels that will not actually be used to maintain a toe-hold in the event of restrictive area licensing, such as that used in Alaska, and to be able to use any other vessels that might be induced to enter the fishery and deliver to the particular cannery.

177

both of which have complicated the regulatory problem without adding significantly to the effectiveness of the industry. It is suggested that the license fees be higher for vessels of greater productivity, though not necessarily proportionately higher.

(3) A revolving fund, serviced out of license revenues, should be set up to permit the state to purchase licenses and gear at a specified percentage of the insurable value of the boat and gear at the option of the owners.[8] Boats purchased under this scheme would be retired or disposed of in such a way that they would not create the same kind of problem in other related fisheries in the Pacific Northwest. Any fisherman relinquishing his license in this fashion would be permitted to re-enter the fishery, but only by purchasing an existing license. Exactly the same avenue into the fishery would be available to any other new entrant.

A voluntary buy-back plan has a number of distinct advantages. By offering an opportunity for some vessel owners to disinvest on a voluntary basis, it would provide some tangible evidence of the effect of gear reduction without imposing hardship on any individual vessel owner. There would undoubtedly be a persistent tendency to retire less efficient units. As vessels and licenses are retired, the value of the remaining licenses will increase since the earning power of individual vessels remaining in the fleet will increase, but this could be offset by an increase in license fees as returns to the fishery improve.

(4) It is suggested that these licenses be made renewable in order to permit the licensee to invest in the necessary boat and gear with reasonable assurance of continued operation. It would be equally essential—to insure flexibility and to provide some pressure to keep the most efficient fishermen in the industry—that licenses be transferable. The prices bid and asked for licenses would also provide a continuing check on the economic condition of the fishery. For purposes of statistical control, and perhaps to exercise some control over flagrant violators of regulations, all license transfer should be handled through the Department of Fisheries.

---

[8] Since most Puget Sound salmon vessels are insured on a cooperative basis, the valuations are considered reliable measures of current market value.

(5) It is suggested that initially the licenses be issued for specified types of gear—purse seine, gill net, and reef net. It would not be wise, however, to freeze the situation permanently. Technological developments and the gear reduction program itself may make it desirable to shift the proportions of the various types of gear. One effective way to accomplish this would be to permit substitution of one type of gear for another on a basis of productivity—i.e., a purse seine license could be acquired by relinquishing a specified number of gill net and/or reef net licenses. It is also possible that the same technique could be used to achieve a gradual shift to improved types of gear without increasing the overall fishing capacity of the industry. Use of a more efficient type of gear would be permitted only with a reduction of a sufficient number of licenses for standard gear to leave fishing capacity unchanged. If the licenses were freely bought and sold, this would permit the introduction of improved types of gear whenever it would be profitable to do so without putting additional pressure on the resource.

It should be stressed that these recommendations, if accepted in principle, provide for step-by-step reduction in fleet size and do not contemplate drastic reductions in the first year or two. It should be noted that even a one-third reduction in gear would provide potential savings ranging from $700,000 to as much as $2.5 million, with an average of perhaps $1.5 million. This would permit substantial increases in incomes to boat-owners and share fishermen and would still provide an annual revenue to the state sufficient to make a buy-back program self-financing.

It is obvious that a gear reduction program of the type outlined above would require a considerable amount of flexibility. It is therefore assumed that any action taken by the legislature would be permissive, with implementation by the Department of Fisheries.

Impact on Other Fisheries. While the program outlined above is relatively straightforward in principle, there are several aspects that require elaboration. One is the impact on other fisheries of a gear reduction program under the framework of the existing

179

treaty organization. One source of immediate concern is the effect on other salmon fisheries in the regulatory area not covered under the treaty. The International Pacific Salmon Fisheries Commission exercises control only over sockeye and pink salmon. Yet, net fishermen also exploit, in the same waters and in overlapping time periods, runs of chinook, silver, and chum salmon. Obviously, these do not go completely unregulated; they are subject to intensive management by the state of Washington and Canada respectively. But, it must be stressed, the programs are not integrated as between the nations. As a result, a serious conflict has arisen between Canadian and American fishermen over the important fisheries for silver salmon now prosecuted by Canadian net fishermen in the Strait of Juan de Fuca and for British Columbia-bound sockeye and pink salmon (mixed with Alaska fish) taken by American fishermen in the vicinity of Noyes Island.

A full discussion of these disputes is beyond the scope of this study.[9] It may simply be noted that Canadian fishermen operating off the mouth of the Strait of Juan de Fuca, under existing restrictions on net fishing geared to the sockeye and pink salmon program, are able to harvest a much larger proportion of the silver stocks that will enter both Puget Sound and British Columbia waters under conditions more favorable to them than to American fishermen (according to the American version). Exactly the reverse situation prevails with respect to the Noyes Island sockeye and pinks (according to the Canadians).

Apart from the matter of equity, which could be negotiable, a more serious threat to the silver stocks results from failure to consider the full impact of fishing effort regulated to achieve desired escapement only for species under the Commission's control. In effect, the industry gears up on the basis of the forecasts and regulations of the Commission, which are derived from its knowledge of the pink and sockeye situation. But this means that the pressure exerted on other species not under its jurisdiction does not enter into the calculation of closed periods or

[9] An analysis of one of the areas in question is available in Martin Nelson and J. A. Crutchfield, *The Straits Silver Fishery*. Report to the Department of Fisheries, State of Washington, 1964 (mimeo).

escapement. While most of the value of both Canadian and American catches from the Puget Sound and Fraser River runs comes from sockeye and pink salmon, it is perfectly conceivable that, in incremental terms, the losses from what is essentially indiscriminate harvesting of silvers and, to a lesser extent, chums and chinooks, would warrant modification of the optimal fishing pattern for the principal species. Certainly inclusion of the silvers is essential if the distinctly undesirable effects of international competition for these fish are to be controlled.

If the gear reduction program outlined above were carried out in Washington (and, possibly, in British Columbia as well) it is essential that steps be taken to prevent a partial shift of the released capacity to other segments of the salmon fishery already in deep difficulties. While it might be possible to eliminate both licenses and gear as indicated above, there is no ready way of eliminating the men, and they are very likely to seek employment in the troll fishery or in Alaska (if the reduction in net fishing is not extended to its salmon operations).

Effect on Industry Structure. In discussion of the proposals outlined above, concern has been expressed about the possibility of complete domination of the Puget Sound salmon fishery by canners. From a purely rational calculation of costs, there is no particular reason to believe that integration of canning and fishing would prove any more attractive under a management program that holds fishing gear to near-optimal levels than it does at present. It is quite possible, however, that the irrational competition for fish by *sub rosa* payments to skippers and subsidized construction of new boats might carry over to an equally unproductive scramble to buy licenses under a restricted-entry fishery. The dominating fear of being cut off from sufficient supplies of fish to assure a minimum degree of utilization of the plant might trigger a move to purchase licenses at prices well above the capitalized value of the potential rent accruing to them. Such a tendency would be strongly reinforced if increased net yields resulting from reduction in excess capacity were not partially absorbed in higher license fees or taxes.

On the other hand, there has always been a hard core of

181

independent fishermen in the Puget Sound salmon fishery, most of them highly competent captain-owners, with a consistent record as "high-liners." If gear reduction were really achieved, the inevitable increases in factor incomes would make it possible, at least, for an independent fishing group to deal at arm's length with all canners while earning opportunity incomes or better. In purely economic terms, of course, it would appear illogical to hold a license in the face of an offer greater than its capitalized claim on future income: but the fisheries (and many other small-scale industries) are full of anomalies of this sort, many of them far less rational. Unless the competition for licenses results in completely outlandish prices, it seems quite possible that the desire for independence, so characteristic of fishermen throughout the world, would lead many of the purse seiners, gill netters, and reef netters to retain their licenses. In more formal economic terms, it may well develop that an independent fishing group, controlling the marginal increment of each year's supply of fish, might be able to extract from the canners a significantly higher price than could otherwise be obtained in the course of pre-season negotiations—the likely method of determining returns to fishermen if the industry were to approach full integration of canning and fishing operations.

On the other side of the fence, canners have expressed equally serious concern over the implications of limited entry for the relative strength of fishermen's organizations in collective bargaining. Despite a series of antitrust cases that appear to outlaw industrywide collective bargaining between salmon fishermen and packers, the practice persists *de facto*. If new entry to the fishery were completely closed, it would certainly provide considerable incentive for full unionization of the industry (or for the formation of effective cooperatives under the Fishery Cooperative Act of 1933, which would permit negotiation of prices with less possibility of problems arising under the antitrust statutes). The industry regards the present situation as open-ended with respect to collective negotiation of prices, and it would be reluctant to give up the possibility of breaking any coordinated effort to forge a really closed bargaining unit among salmon fishermen.

We are much less concerned about the validity of these arguments than about the fervor with which they are advanced and the apparent proclivity of crucial portions of the industry to "rather bear those ills we have than fly to others that we know not of." It is by no means clear, for example, that integration of fishing and processing, partial or complete, would have any adverse effect on the administrative efficiency of the regulatory agencies. On the contrary, we would expect some improvement in compliance and in the speed and accuracy of information provided to the Commission. In addition, integration of all or a substantial part of the industry would permit it to do legally what must now be done *sub rosa* with respect to pre-season determination of prices to be paid for fish.[10] Perhaps the most compelling argument against any serious unforeseen effects from further integration of the industry is the fact that it is, from an economic standpoint, already an accomplished fact; only a small number of boats are free of substantial packer control through indebtedness.

What of the public interest? Would either integration or the development of much stronger bargaining units in the fishing fleets result in higher prices or lower quality? It is difficult to see what unfavorable repercussions could result from rationalization in the fishery along the lines suggested. Any price effects would be neutral or favorable. Given consumer demand for the several end products involved, the price of salmon to consumers is determined once the regulatory authority has indicated the amount that can be taken. Within any single season, the quantity taken is almost completely insensitive to prices (at least over ranges that have prevailed over the last three decades). The public has no particular interest in procedures or mechanisms involved in pre-retail distribution of these proceeds unless it can be demonstrated that they restrict total output to levels lower than those permitted under existing regulatory standards. To the best of our knowledge, this has never occurred in the salmon fishery, even in areas where buying power is heavily concentrated.

In addition, it should not be impossible to devise legal safe-

---

[10] The issues involved here are discussed in detail in J. A. Crutchfield "Fishermen's Union and the Anti-Trust Statutes: The Economic Issues," *Industrial and Labor Relations Review, VIII*, 4:531–36, July 1955.

guards that would minimize direct participation by packers in the fishery if it were deemed desirable to do so. Obviously, some evasion would always be possible, but concern over "monopoly" in this rather obscure sense could be laid to rest through appropriate legislative action if, in some manner not now apparent, integration should result in a continuing undue restriction of output.

Gear Reduction and the Sport Fishery. In all the Pacific Coast salmon areas except Alaska, the relationship between commercial and sport fishing must be taken into consideration in any overall control program. In Washington, for example, the number of salmon anglers is currently estimated at more than 400,000 and in recent years fishing effort has averaged about a million angler days per year. A small number of pinks—50,000 to 90,000 in recent years—are taken by Washington sportsmen, but the real clash between recreational and commercial usage centers on chinooks and cohoes.

In many respects, however, the conflict is more apparent than real. Net-caught chinook and coho salmon account for only about 10 percent of the total value taken in Puget Sound waters, and the peak of the commercial net fishery for silver salmon occurs after virtually all sport fishing has ceased. The light recreational pressure on the peak and latter parts of the silver runs is due in large part to their timing; the fish are moving rapidly, often in deeper water, after Labor Day, when both available recreation time and weather conditions cut sharply into sport fishing effort. It has been estimated that as much as 80 percent of the sport catch of mature cohoes inside the Strait of Juan de Fuca is taken from the first 15 percent of the run.[11] The really serious conflict between sport and commercial fishermen in Washington centers on the trollers; and the real public issue is that at present neither group is subject to effective regulation.

For purposes of this study, two points might be stressed. First, greater efficiency in management, achieved by a substantial reduction in the number of units of the commercial net fishery,

[11] Personal communication from J. S. Lasater, Department of Fisheries, State of Washington, 1966.

184

would reduce pressure on the species that are important to sport fishermen. Second, an integrated management program should be extended to include both sport fishermen and the trolling fleet if the coho and chinook stocks are to be harvested efficiently.

Factor Mobility. The gear reduction program recommended above takes specific account of the problems posed by immobility of both labor and capital in the commercial fisheries. Quite apart from the legal ramifications, no one could recommend in good conscience a method of gear reduction that imposed serious capital losses on those who had invested in good faith or that raised a threat of a compulsory shift in employment to a labor force already well over the average age for employed workers in the region. The concept of a voluntary buy-back system, accompanied by a flat prohibition on issuance of new licenses, makes it possible to accomplish at least part of the necessary reduction in inputs on a purely voluntary basis. Whatever steps might have to be taken thereafter to encourage further exit, particularly to permit the introduction of new and more efficient techniques, the program would then be well enough established to permit an assessment of both costs and methods of alleviating the threat of individual hardship. It must be reiterated that the present age distribution of both men and vessels in the Pacific Coast fisheries in general is such that the mere closure of entry will result in considerable attrition within a rather short period of time.

As far as Washington is concerned, growth rates of the regional economy and the dominant position in the fishery of men of American and Scandinavian origin suggests that the problem of absorbing young recruits who would otherwise have entered the fishery would not be severe. The numbers involved are simply too small to affect the general labor market, and the groups involved are in no sense culturally or economically underprivileged. There is, however, a mild problem in Washington that grows to really serious proportions in Alaska and in British Columbia: the heavy reliance of some Indian tribes on salmon fishing, and the fact that they are—in geographic, cultural, and economic terms—highly immobile. A preferred position for Indian fishermen in any gear reduction program would involve only a trifling

185

concession to efficiency in Washington, but in some parts of Alaska and British Columbia it raises the possibility that a disproportionately large part of the total catch would go to the least efficient units in the fishery.

As in all problems dealing with structural immobility arising out of unequal economic opportunity, there are no easy short-run answers. It is suggested, however, that there are more efficient ways to provide better economic opportunity for isolated Indian groups than to maintain them in an inefficient fishery incapable of generating either means or incentive for change.

Recommended Gear Reduction Program: Alaska

It goes without saying that the complexity of the Alaska salmon fisheries would require some modification of the program outlined for Puget Sound, though the essential approach is equally applicable. Fortunately, this is also true for more conventional concepts of regulation. The Alaskan fisheries have been subdivided into smaller geographic units for management purposes for many years, and the same units could be used to advantage in framing policies for improved economic efficiency.

In Bristol Bay, where virtually all fish are taken with a single type of gear, a simple gear reduction program of the Puget Sound type could be applied in straightforward fashion. The only real difficulty might come in the allocation of licenses between resident Alaskan fishermen on the one hand, and cannery-owned units operated by non-resident fishermen on the other. There is no doubt that there would be great political pressure in Alaska to throw the burden of the adjustment on "the outsiders." If this sentiment could be overcome, overall efficiency suggests that a parallel reduction would be more acceptable. If not, there might be serious questions as to the legality of a gear reduction procedure that discriminates in favor of state residents.

The same comments would apply to any gear reduction program in other parts of Alaska, with additional complication imposed by the need to allocate the reduced number of licenses by type of gear. As in Puget Sound, a parallel reduction in gear of various types probably imposes small costs in efficiency terms, and would have the virtue of a rough sort of equity. Again, insistence on preferred status for residents of the state would present a more formidable obstacle. The problem of special treatment to Indians in all parts of Alaska has already been mentioned in the previous section.

During the initial phases of any scheme to reduce excessive fishing capacity, it might be necessary and desirable to continue, at least for some period of time, the present Alaska technique of area licensing, under which vessels must register in advance for particular fishing areas, and may not thereafter fish in other areas in a given season. After the worst of the pressure has been relieved, however, it should be possible to restore a greater degree of interregional flexibility without running a grave risk of excessive concentrations of gear at any single point—a situation which brought about the use of area restrictions.

We are keenly aware of the fact that in any effort at rationalization of the Alaska salmon fisheries obstacles of a political or administrative nature are no less formidable than those that involve more fundamental conceptual difficulties. A realistic appraisal of the Alaskan situation suggests that it might be necessary to settle, initially, for a simple prohibition against further increases in the number of licensed units. Lest this be considered an inconsequential step, let it be remembered that if such a restriction had been in effect after World War II, Alaskan catches probably would be larger than they are today, and a very substantial net economic yield would be available as additional incomes to fishermen and as a means of financing research and development in the fisheries. Looking at the Pacific Coast fisheries as a whole, there is little reason to believe that the aggregate physical output of salmon can be increased very substantially. Gains from restoration of the depleted runs in Alaska are likely to be offset, at least partially, by the increasing inroads of population and industrial growth throughout the Pacific Coast. The real price of salmon may therefore be expected to continue upward; and if nothing else could be accomplished, it would be worthwhile to prevent the inevitable increase in economic waste that would otherwise result from these rising prices.

The practical politics of fishery regulation in both Alaska and Washington suggest the urgency of a thorough analysis of the specific impact on specific industry groups of alternative methods of gear limitation. Discussions to date indicate the importance of one obstacle that can be overcome: uncertainty over the allocation of gains (and compensating losses) attributable to an effective gear reduction program; and, because of that uncertainty, a general unwillingness to disclose essential information for fear it would help a rival group. The essential mutuality of interests in a more efficient fishery must be demonstrated in concrete terms before there can be any real hope of progress.

Data Requirements

Data relating to factor earnings and the economic efficiency of operating units are almost nonexistent. Since regulation geared entirely to biological objectives has been forced to rely on reduction in gear efficiency, even the yield-effort data that can be gleaned from the operating records of fishing units are virtually meaningless in terms of *attainable* costs. It is highly desirable, whether or not the gear restriction program is implemented, that procedures be developed to measure the economic performance of the industry on a continuing basis. The Puget Sound salmon and the halibut studies indicate that regular sampling of operating data from accounting records and direct surveys of earnings of fishermen could provide, fairly easily, an acceptably accurate index of factor earnings. These data, together with market prices at which restricted licenses are transferred, would also provide an essential test of the impact of reduction in excess capacity.

In addition, a long-run rationalization program would call for detailed studies of the physical productivity of different types of salmon fishing gear by area as a first step toward delineation of optimal combinations of gear at different levels of fishing effort. A decade ago this would have been considered a hopelessly complex problem, involving simultaneous solution of thousands of equations in a sequential process. However, in salmon fishing areas where adequate past data on the timing of runs and catches can be pieced together, modern computer techniques make it possible to simulate the entire physical setting of the fishery and to evaluate a large number of alternative combinations. Once developed and tested, a computer model would cost very little to use for this and a variety of other purposes in a management program concerned with both physical and economic variables.[12]

RESEARCH AND DEVELOPMENT

It is difficult to avoid the conclusion that if the fishery remains on an open access basis, the potential benefits from government and university research directed specifically at applied aspects of salmon production and harvesting simply cannot be realized, except for the value one chooses to place on the accretion of scientific knowledge for its own sake. Any improvement in physical output per unit of input, any expansion of aggregate production through more intensive use of spawning areas or artificial propagation, any improvements in processing or marketing technology that produce increased income will be dissipated in new entry. It is perhaps in partial (and unacknowledged) recognition of this fact that much research on Pacific salmon appears to veer off in directions that have little immediate or even long-run application to economic utilization of the fish.

If, however, even partial limitation of salmon gear could be achieved—say, by a moratorium on additional inputs in the fisheries—returns from expanded research would appear to be most attractive. In particular, the critical problem of forecasting each year's runs with greater accuracy promises real improvement in the economic efficiency of the industry as well as in the long-run impact on productivity of the stocks of more selective and accurate calculation of escapements. In the more remote parts of Alaska, where virtually all costs must be committed in advance, and where the present reliance on area restrictions will continue, it is vitally important that forecasting be improved. This is, of course, no secret, and effective cooperative effort along precisely these lines is being undertaken by federal, state, international, and university research personnel. But the budget available for this work is pitifully small; it must be greatly expanded in ex-

---

[12] A general summary of data requirements for management programs geared to net economic yield is outlined in an unpublished report of a Food and Agriculture Organization of the United Nations meeting convened to consider the matter in September 1965. For the methodology involved in constructing models of salmon fisheries for computer analysis see Royce *et al., op. cit.,* Part III and appendix.

pensive areas, such as those required for integration of fishery and oceanographic work on the high seas, if really significant improvements are to be achieved. Recognition of the need for more research and of the visible and attractive economic payoff that would result makes it even more imperative that some of the necessary financial support be made available by more efficient use of the resource itself.

It is heartening that both federal and state fishery agencies are undertaking analyses of the internal consistency of salmon enhancement programs, using modern benefit-cost techniques. "Operation Fin Clip" and "Operation Coho," initiated in 1962 and 1966 respectively by the Bureau of Commercial Fisheries, should provide definitive answers as to the economic contribution of its Columbia River hatchery program, and similar analyses of hatchery and natural rearing programs have been initiated by all of the Pacific Coast states and by British Columbia. In conjunction with continuing efforts to coordinate salmon research among state, federal, and university agencies, these projects hold out real promise for improved productivity of public investment in salmon stocks.

The Japanese High-Seas Fishery

Thus far our recommended program for regulation of the Pacific salmon fisheries has assumed participation only by American and Canadian fishermen, with internationally shared salmon fisheries subject to regulation under treaty. We must now take account of the existence and possible extension of Japanese participation in the fishery—and perhaps of entry by other nations in the future.

The history of conflict over the North Pacific high-seas fisheries is far too lengthy even to summarize here.[13] With respect to salmon, the Japanese fishery has rested historically on limited runs in the northern Japanese islands and, much more exten-

[13] A thorough discussion may be found in Richard Van Cleve and Ralph W. Johnson, *Management of the High Seas Fisheries of the Northeastern Pacific*, University of Washington Publications in Fisheries, New Series, Vol. II, No. 2, 1963; Francis T. Christy, Jr. and Anthony Scott, *The Common Wealth in Ocean Fisheries* (Baltimore: The Johns Hopkins Press, 1966).

sively, on Asian stocks destined for Siberian rivers. Before World War II, some exploratory fishing activity had been undertaken in the vicinity of 175 degrees west longitude (the boundary roughly demarcating Asian and North American stocks), but limited commercial fishing off the Alaska coast in the late 1930's was halted after vigorous diplomatic protests.

After World War II, a treaty was negotiated by Japan, Canada, and the United States under which Japanese high-seas fishing activity was expressly prohibited east of 175 degrees west longitude.[14] The treaty was essentially an expression of the American principle of "abstention," based on the proposition that fully exploited stocks, subject to scientific management by the countries that had developed them, should not be open to entry by other nations. It was believed that the line as drawn effectively precluded Japanese exploitation of North American salmon, halibut, or herring stocks, of concern to both Canadian and American fishermen.

The treaty was ratified in 1953, and was to run for ten years, after which it could be terminated unilaterally by any of the three signatory nations after 12 months' notice. The Soviet Union has never been included in the treaty. Apart from the definition of the "abstention" stocks and areas, work of the International North Pacific Fisheries Commission, created under the treaty, has been confined almost entirely to scientific investigations. Its objectives were to increase knowledge of the ocean phase of the life history of the Pacific salmon and to determine areas in which Asian and North American stocks intermingle, with primary emphasis on the area in the vicinity of the line. The Commission has no authority to regulate fishing activity, nor is it concerned in its investigations with economic aspects of the fishing operation or with specific conflicts of interest among the participating nations relating to incompatible gear or the division of the catch from jointly exploited stocks.

[14] The text of the treaty, as amended to 1965, may be found in *Treaties and Other International Agreements Containing Provisions on Commercial Fisheries, Marine Resources, Sport Fisheries, and Wildlife to which the United States is a Party*, Committee on Commerce, United States Senate, 89th Congress, 1st Session, 1965, pp. 76–86.

Subsequent investigations have indicated that there is considerable mingling of stocks in the North Pacific. The fact that some Asian fish were found east of the critical line was of no significance, since neither Canadian nor American salmon fishermen operate on the high seas.[15] But it also became clear that Bristol Bay red salmon regularly migrated west of the line and were being exploited by Japanese high-seas fishing vessels. As a result, a steadily mounting clamor has arisen in the United States and Canada, protesting Japanese capture of fish originating in North American rivers, and (in the case of American fishing interests) threatening reprisals of various sorts unless the Japanese fishery were terminated or the abstention line pushed farther westward to eliminate the operation.

From a world standpoint, there can be no doubt that harvesting Pacific salmon on the high seas is woefully inefficient on three counts. First, there is obviously a waste of capital and labor involved in the high-seas operation itself, since it cannot be as efficient as a fishery harvesting the fish as they approach the spawning streams near operating bases and in concentrated groups. Secondly, all Pacific salmon grow rapidly during the last period before the spawning runs begin; a high-seas fishery sacrifices a considerable amount of weight for relatively little offset in the way of reduced natural mortality. Finally, it makes it impossible to manage individual runs. On the other hand, the glaring waste of the high-seas fishery relative to optimal harvesting implies nothing as to its desirability from the standpoint of the Japanese. Without an open-sea operation they would get no North American salmon,[16] and it seems apparent that profits from the fishery, foreign exchange considerations, or both, indicate the desirability of continuing it. It may be, of course, that the rising pressure of general wage increases in Japan, already felt acutely in other Japanese distant water fisheries, may ultimately pinch off the North Pacific salmon operation, but to await such developments hardly seems a satisfactory way of resolving

---

15 At present, both Canada and the United States prohibit net fishing for salmon in the ocean beyond the surf line.

16 An additional avenue is through Japanese acquisition of equity positions in American or Canadian firms.

the complex issues involved. The Japanese have been harvesting Asian salmon at sea for a long period of time, and their present techniques, using mother ships and catcher boats that set gill nets a mile to a mile and a half in length, are apparently capable of production costs approaching those of more conventional shore-based fisheries in both the United States and the Soviet Union.

We conclude that in the absence of any change in the present situation, the possibility of managing the Bristol Bay fishery in anything approaching optimal fashion would be seriously jeopardized by continuation of the Japanese open-sea effort. Fortunately, the bulk of the Alaska, British Columbia, and Puget Sound salmon catches would not be affected, since migration beyond (westward of) 175° west longitude by species originating in other areas of the Pacific Coast does not appear to be of major importance. It must be remembered, however, that the treaty is now being continued on a year-to-year basis. If negotiations among the three nations concerned were to break down completely (or if the Soviet Union, China, or South Korea should initiate uncontrolled salmon fishing on the high seas), the threat of catastrophic damage to all the North Pacific salmon fisheries would become real indeed. Open-sea gill net fishing, as now practiced by the Japanese, could be made murderously effective operating outside the three (or twelve) mile limit. If some appropriate agreement could not be reached very quickly, the situation with respect to salmon management would degenerate rapidly.

From the Japanese standpoint, the 1953 treaty is regarded as basically unfair on two grounds: it was imposed on the Japanese during a period when they were in no position to bargain at arm's length; and the Japanese hold that it contravenes generally accepted principles of international law regarding freedom of the high seas. Since the abstention principle is not generally recognized elsewhere in the world, it is likely that world opinion might support the Japanese claim for some measure of participation in the salmon fisheries of North America as well as Asia on the grounds of historic rights, economic need, or some other basis equally hard to counter from the standpoint of conservation of the salmon stocks—particularly when the American and

Canadian conservation program is shot through with economic inefficiency. It is difficult to overlook the fact that the treaty, as now worded, really offers nothing to the Japanese except a prohibition—in terms of domestic policies, an almost untenable position for their negotiators.

If Japanese participation should appear essential to preventing a complete breakdown in salmon management, it is probable that the national quota device would be the most effective, at least as an initial step. This would at least permit some degree of planning in the Bristol Bay forecasting and management program, and might obviate the unenticing necessity of extending multilateral international management to all of the fisheries of the North Pacific Coast. It would not, of course, prevent dissipation of potential net economic yield unless accompanied by some restriction on inputs.

CHAPTER 11

Conclusions

~~~~~~

The conclusions that emerge from these case studies of fisheries management in Pacific Coast salmon industry are sobering indeed. In spite of millions of dollars poured into research, propagation, and regulatory activity, the resource is, at best, holding its own and in some areas is clearly subject to continuing depletion. Even in the few cases where stocks have been rebuilt, such as the Fraser River sockeye, the evidence is overwhelming that potential gains from the scientific and regulatory program have been largely if not entirely dissipated through excessive factor cost resulting from the inability to appropriate the economic rent that would accrue, under rational exploitation, to the owner—private or public—of the basic resource.

Failure to cope with the economic reaction of the industry to rising real prices of salmon and to the mechanics of the control programs employed has resulted in serious deterioration of actual, as compared to potential, physical yield from the resource—partly because of unbalanced cropping of sub-segments of the major stocks exploited. In attempts to stave off complete disaster, the regulatory authorities, both state and international,

195

have been forced to resort to progressively more stringent restrictions on the efficiency of the gear and vessels employed. To some extent this merely carries forward the conglomerate mass of regulations inherited from the past, much of it written when public action had little footing in scientific knowledge. More often it represented the net result of power plays by the competing fishing and processing groups involved. Even more disturbing is the degree to which necessity has become confused with virtue. A discouragingly large proportion of those connected with salmon research and regulatory programs regard reductions in efficiency as not only necessary but desirable in the present setting. The ability to achieve a given reduction in sweep efficiency of the fleet as a whole, coupled with the convenient ability to shrug off responsibility for economic side effects, has contributed to a surprisingly complacent attitude toward trends in regulation that continuously undermine the competitive strength of the salmon industry.

As long as the present situation continues, there can be no real hope of economic health in the fishery. Any increase in relative prices of salmon is promptly swallowed up by increased entry, rising costs, and more stringent pressure on the physical resource and those charged with its management. It simply leads to a new equilibrium, no more satisfactory than the previous one, with a net loss to the economy as a whole as more factors of production are trapped in the fishery. Moreover, the inexorable logic of the unrestricted entry situation suggests that the industry will always be balanced on the razor's edge with respect to interindustry and international competition.

In brief, the generalized model of Chapter 2 works as *a priori* reasoning suggests it will. In actual fact, however, the situation in the salmon industry is somewhat worse than the model would suggest, since no formal bio-economic theory can deal with the additional complications introduced by the inefficiency imposed by the regulatory process, and the debilitating effect on the management program engendered by the deep entanglement of the industry in state, national, and international politics. In addition, the familiar asymmetry between entry and exit conditions leads to a greater degree of overcapacity and lower factor returns than the long-run model predicts—particularly when labor mobility is as restricted as it is in the salmon fishery in Alaska. Though we have considered only the Puget Sound and Alaska fisheries in detail, the California, Columbia River, and British Columbia fisheries do not differ in any significant respect.

Is this dismal performance limited to the salmon industry and is it rooted in any peculiar characteristics of that particular fishery? We think not. A review of the literature suggests that precisely the same results have been realized in other fisheries of quite different biological and structural characteristics, and that the key element accounting for the pattern of performance noted in this study operates in others as well.[1]

The study of the Pacific halibut fishery,[2] for example, dealt with an operation geared to the exploitation of a slow-growing demersal fish, sedentary in nature, and taken with one type of gear. The fishery could be exploited over most if not all of the calendar year. Regulation, when it came, took the form of tight quota control, coupled with a complete proscription of all but one approved type of gear. In short, the characteristics of the exploited stock and the mechanics of both fishing and regulation were very different than those encountered in the salmon fishery. Yet the results, for all practical purposes, were identical. A rapid increase in real prices of halibut, together with a substantial recovery in the magnitude of the stocks—both numbers and average size of fish—brought a surge of new entrants into the industry, particularly in the immediate postwar period. In addition to the expected dissipation of economic rent in excess capacity, a variety of secondary effects stemming from the profit-maximizing reactions to the control program brought further increases in costs. These adjustments include: the necessary shortening of the fishing season; use of combination boats able to fish several types of gear in order to permit reasonably full utilization of the hull and engine; non-optimal geographical distribution of landing

[1] A broad review of the literature, with special emphasis on international fisheries, is presented in Francis T. Christy, Jr. and Anthony Scott, *The Common Wealth in Ocean Fisheries* (Baltimore: The Johns Hopkins Press, 1966).

[2] J. A. Crutchfield and Arnold Zellner, *Economic Aspects of the Pacific Halibut Fishery,* Fishery Industrial Research, Vol. 1 (Washington: U.S. Department of the Interior, 1961).

facilities; and some increase in marketing costs and loss of quality as a result of longer storage periods.

As in the salmon case, the necessity of adapting to sub-optimal types of capital equipment factor combinations and geographic distribution of effort resulted in a series of structural changes in both the fishery and the processing-marketing sector that tend to become self-perpetuating. The halibut industry has become, to a somewhat lesser degree than the salmon industry but still significantly, an employer of casual, part-time laborers, many of whom draw substantial unemployment compensation even during good years. There is inevitable waste of irreplaceable man-hours of potential labor time in unnecessary job shifting. The success of the halibut program in a biological sense has very little effect on the net economic yield from the fishery. In the absence of any means or authority to maximize the economic contribution from the operation and thus to restrict entry, the economic benefit to the community as a whole is almost certain to be very slight or zero, except under conditions of less than full employment of factors utilized in the fishery in question. Precisely the same comments apply to the salmon fishery.

A study of the New England bottom-fishing industry by a group of Boston College economists[3] yielded essentially the same conclusions although the purposes of the analysis were somewhat different and it was not carried through to the same conclusion with respect to potential gains from limitations of factor inputs. The only regulation affecting this fishery in significant degree is a mesh-size limitation (which presumably prevents the capture of uneconomically small fish). But any gains in yield per unit of effort from this partial shift to eumetric yield functions are promptly wiped out by increased inputs. The conclusion seems warranted that the economic performance of an intensively exploited fishery, as far as returns to individual units and overall economic efficiency are concerned, will be about the same regardless of whether it is regulated or not, provided the rate of

---

[3] E. J. Lynch, R. M. Doherty, and G. P. Draheim, *The Groundfish Industries of New England and Canada*. U.S. Fish and Wildlife Service, Circular 121, Washington, 1961.

exploitation is below levels that threaten the existence of the basic stocks.[4]

There is mounting evidence that even the massive fish stocks of the North Atlantic are coming under sufficient pressure to yield the same kind of results. The tremendous increase in fishing capacity of the North Atlantic countries, bolstered by a huge expansion of modern Russian fishing fleets, may well have reached a point where severe overfishing, at least in the economic sense used in this study, is already upon us.[5] It is intriguing to note that the long-range development plan for the Polish fisheries takes specific cognizance of the inevitability of depletion on the North Atlantic grounds and calls for development of types of vessels capable of extending their operations to the southeast and southwest Atlantic within the foreseeable future.

There is also increasing concern about the incompatibility of expansion plans on the productive bottom fisheries of the North African coast. At present more than 200 oceangoing trawlers are operating on these stocks, and the higher-valued species, capable of being fished selectively to some degree, are already showing signs of wear and tear. The ubiquitous tendency to generalize overcapacity in marine fisheries is highlighted dramatically by the fact that even a country as small as Ghana is now attempting to activate a fleet of 48 modern high-seas draggers capable of fishing both the North African grounds and those lying south of the Congo River.

[4] Similar results were obtained in a recent study of the Norwegian Winter Herring Fishery. See G. Pontecorvo and K. Vartdal, Jr., "Optimizing Resource Use: The Norwegian Winter Herring Fishery," in *Statsøkonomisk Tidsskrift*, #2, 1967. In addition, there is strong evidence that the Peruvian *Anchoveta* (fishmeal) fishery is moving rapidly in this direction. See G. Pontecorvo and J. Townsend, "The Conditions of the Peruvian Fishmeal Industry: Including Recommendations for Policy Action" (Lima: United Nations Industrial Development Organization, June 28, 1968).

[5] The International Commission for the Northwest Atlantic Fisheries and the International Commission for the Northeast Atlantic Fisheries are currently conducting inquiries into alternative methods of regulating cod and haddock catches, on the ground that all North Atlantic stocks of these important species, with the possible exception of those in the Labrador area, are being exploited at or very near levels of maximum physical yield.

The conclusion is clear. In this study we have dealt in some detail with a localized fishery of unique biological characteristics to demonstrate the inevitability of overfishing, under appropriate economic stimuli with respect to costs and prices, and the essential futility of efforts to achieve an optimal fishery through control programs defined only in physical terms. But there is no reason to doubt that the problem is completely general, differing only in the degree of seriousness and the speed with which the depletion process will develop wherever price-cost relationships are favorable. It must be borne in mind that high-seas fishing, partly because of the inexorable inroads on established fish stocks, has undergone a revolutionary expansion in range and potential sweep efficiency. There is hardly a body of salt water in the world that cannot be fished economically, at least in the initial phases, by vessels of any nation.

Obviously, the world will not come to an end if its fishery resources are abused in this fashion. As Scott has pointed out,[6] the importance of the fisheries, both as a source of protein food and as an engine for economic development in emerging economies, has probably been more consistently overstated than understated. Nevertheless, efficient exploitation of resources on a global basis depends on using each component wisely. We cannot look with anything but dismay on a series of developments, each flying in the face of past experience and each contributing to a hardening set of international conventions geared to inadequate concepts of conservation and management of fishery resources. This study is simply symptomatic of a general problem of really serious proportions.

Unfortunately, there are no simple remedies, though our analysis—like that of Scott, Gordon, Christy, Sinclair, and Turvey—indicates that the principles at issue are not complex. As in the case of North American agriculture, the key problems in achieving better economic performance lie in "how" rather than "why" or "what." Variations in the geographic, technical, legal, and sociological elements underlying the structure of different

[6] Anthony Scott, "Fisheries Development and National Economic Development," *Proceedings of the Gulf and Caribbean Fisheries Institute*, Eighteenth Annual Session, November 1965.

fisheries call for careful construction of efficiency-oriented management programs adapted to each separate case. In almost every instance the process of change is inhibited in speed and precision by the necessity of "unscrambling eggs." Once the industry has adjusted to depletion and/or to regulations framed in terms of physical objectives, second-best solutions are the best one can hope for, at least in the short run. There is no record of a major fishery management scheme that was not introduced in an atmosphere of desperation after the evidence of severe depletion had become too obvious for any explanation other than over-fishing. The difficulties are compounded where fisheries are exploited by both market-oriented and socialist nations and by countries with radically different cost-and-demand patterns.

Our deep concern that steps be taken to rationalize salmon management reflects our belief that the first successful steps to improve economic results from regulatory programs will exert a far wider influence for good, in international as well as national fishery circles. The difficulties are real in the case of salmon, but the size of the gap between the high prices of end products and the fishing costs that can be achieved with present technical knowledge offers the possibility of a striking demonstration of the practical importance of attention to the economics of regulation.

Appendix Tables

Table A–1. Landings and Values, Alaska Salmon, 1927–67

Year	Landings (thousand pounds)	Value (thousand dollars)
1927	300,566	$ 8,702
1928	517,069	12,790
1929	442,602	10,844
1930	426,442	8,041
1931	467,664	7,758
1932	452,536	5,766
1933	467,349	7,498
1934	624,651	9,881
1935	434,004	6,969
1936	726,853	11,857
1937	593,384	11,876
1938	589,706	9,943
1939	452,166	9,256
1940	439,182	8,420
1941	543,024	12,609
1942	430,867	13,398
1943	457,307	14,588
1944	393,318	14,527
1945	402,635	15,564
1946	391,689	17,089
1947	381,808	19,570
1948	338,370	23,144
1949	388,345	32,662
1950	264,919	22,637
1951	276,588	32,368
1952	282,967	31,020
1953	220,276	21,498
1954	247,033	24,597
1955	203,675	21,615
1956	269,898	29,752
1957	203,437	25,036
1958	241,255	26,847
1959	147,280	20,956
1960	207,101	33,556
1961	264,814	35,741
1962	277,848	42,119
1963	223,063	31,298
1964	311,623	41,359
1965	274,844	48,274
1966	333,325	54,202
1967 (prelim.)	131,000	24,800

Source: Fishery Statistics of the United States, U.S. Department of the Interior, Fish and Wildlife Service, Bureau of Commercial Fisheries.

Table A–2. Current-dollar and Real Prices to Salmon Fishermen in Alaska:
Sockeye, Pink, and All Salmon, 1935–67

(cents per pound)

Year	Sockeye		Pink		All salmon	
	Current	Real	Current	Real	Current	Real
1935	2.6	6.2	1.4	3.3	1.6	3.8
1936	2.4	5.6	1.3	3.1	1.6	3.8
1937	2.8	6.3	1.6	3.6	2.0	4.5
1938	2.1	5.1	1.4	3.4	1.7	4.1
1939	2.7	6.8	1.7	4.3	2.0	5.0
1940	2.9	7.2	1.7	4.2	1.9	4.7
1941	2.5	5.7	2.2	5.0	2.3	5.2
1942	4.2	8.1	3.0	5.8	3.1	6.0
1943	3.9	6.7	2.5	4.3	3.2	5.5
1944	4.6	8.1	3.1	5.4	3.7	6.5
1945	4.4	7.5	2.8	4.8	3.9	6.7
1946	4.6	6.9	3.9	5.8	4.4	6.6
1947	5.1	6.3	4.2	5.2	5.1	6.3
1948	6.3	7.1	6.2	7.0	6.8	7.7
1949	7.9	9.3	8.5	10.0	8.4	9.9
1950	8.4	9.8	7.8	9.1	8.4	9.8
1951	11.5	12.0	11.5	12.0	11.7	12.2
1952	11.7	12.0	9.4	9.7	11.0	11.3
1953	11.7	12.2	8.2	8.6	9.8	10.3
1954	12.5	13.1	8.9	9.3	10.0	10.4
1955	12.9	13.7	8.8	9.4	10.6	11.3
1956	14.8	15.6	9.0	9.5	11.0	11.6
1957	16.2	16.5	10.8	11.0	12.3	12.4
1958	18.2	17.8	9.1	8.9	11.1	10.8
1959	19.0	18.9	10.5	10.4	14.2	14.1
1960	20.4	20.1	13.0	12.8	16.2	15.9
1961	18.4	17.9	9.8	9.6	13.5	13.1
1962	21.0	20.2	14.2	13.7	15.2	14.6
1963	21.6	20.5	11.7	11.1	14.0	13.3
1964	22.6	21.2	10.6	9.9	13.3	12.5
1965	21.7	19.9	10.3	9.4	17.6	16.1
1966	21.3	18.6	13.6	11.9	16.3	14.2
1967	21.0	18.0	13.1	11.2	18.9	16.2

Source: Fishery Statistics of the United States, U.S. Department of the Interior, Fish and Wildlife Service, Bureau of Commercial Fisheries.

Deflator: Consumer Price Index, Bureau of Labor Statistics (All Foods). 1957–59 = 100.

Table A–3. Number of Fishermen and Average Catch per Fisherman, Alaska Salmon Fishery, 1927–66

Year	Number of fishermen	Average catch (pounds)
1927	8,007	37,571
1928	8,627	57,452
1929	8,208	55,325
1930	7,408	60,920
1931	6,767	66,809
1932	5,922	75,423
1933	6,515	66,763
1934	7,351	89,236
1935	7,026	62,001
1936	9,516	72,685
1937	9,372	65,932
1938	8,651	65,523
1939	9,242	50,241
1940	7,553	54,898
1941	8,003	67,878
1942	7,528	53,858
1943	7,802	57,163
1944	7,800	49,165
1945	6,962	57,519
1946	8,572	43,521
1947	10,234	38,181
1948	10,014	33,837
1949	8,874	43,149
1950	9,343	29,435
1951	11,504	23,049
1952	12,691	21,767
1953	12,175	18,356
1954	10,628	22,458
1955	12,004	16,973
1956	11,666	22,492
1957	10,713	18,494
1958	11,214	21,932
1959	10,339	14,728
1960	11,919	17,258
1961	14,010	16,786
1962	16,405	16,661
1963	17,867	12,485
1964	17,211	18,106
1965	14,214	19,336
1966	17,765	18,763

Source: Annual reports of the Bureau of Commercial Fisheries and its predecessor agencies.

Table A–4. *Major Operating Units in Alaska Salmon Fishery, 1927–65*

Year	Purse seines (fathoms)	Gill nets (fathoms)
1927	81,663	295,622
1928	91,394	296,607
1929	98,308	284,005
1930	93,654	256,465
1931	65,123	250,973
1932	39,795	189,720
1933	59,345	214,847
1934	76,445	222,586
1935	114,300	131,794
1936	118,705	289,795
1937	118,826	289,550
1938	97,310	312,903
1939	104,463	332,687
1940	113,265	245,445
1941	109,893	268,667
1942	142,250	202,485
1943	102,345	221,950
1944	115,141	273,445
1945	122,330	218,730
1946	141,108	311,555
1947	141,655	399,606
1948	115,720	461,982
1949	109,798	421,662
1950	122,961	448,901
1951	150,458	573,402
1952	162,471	613,590
1953	152,384	640,955
1954	136,279	575,370
1955	171,931	705,178
1956	217,821	655,215
1957	197,160	842,650
1958	216,006	759,000
1959	188,270	636,135
1960	285,923	559,444
1961	249,493	641,945
1962	281,500	688,850
1963	312,500	715,500
1964	288,000	755,500
1965	284,000	778,000

Source: Annual reports of the Bureau of Commercial Fisheries and its predecessor agencies.

Table A-5. Bristol Bay Catch, 1893-1967

(thousands of fish)

Year	Catch[a]	Year	Catch[a]
1893–99[b]	3,821	1946	8,051
1900–04[b]	11,960	1947	18,662
1905–09[b]	13,516	1948	14,544
1910–14[b]	15,576	1949	6,449
1915–19[b]	17,415	1950	7,157
1920–24[b]	15,339	1951	4,326
1925–29[b]	14,059	1952	11,266
1930	4,259	1953	6,112
1931	12,790	1954	4,640
1932	14,940	1955	4,483
1933	23,709	1956	8,744
1934	20,601	1957	6,325
1935	3,068	1958	2,949
1936	20,587	1959	4,494
1937	21,252	1960	13,705
1938	24,700	1961	11,914
1939	13,331	1962	4,731
1940	4,727	1963	3,345
1941	7,154	1964	8,106
1942	6,343	1965	25,218
1943	17,330	1966	9,314
1944	11,545	1967	4,184
1945	7,300		

[a] Includes both drift and set net catch.

[b] Annual average.

Source: (1893–1927) W. Rich and E. Ball, *Statistical Review of the Alaska Salmon Fisheries, Part I: Bristol Bay and Alaska Peninsula.* Bulletin of U.S. Bureau of Fisheries, Vol. XLIV, p. 57. (1928–59) Olie Matheson, Fisheries Research Institute, University of Washington. (1960–67) *Fishery Statistics of the United States,* U.S. Department of the Interior, Fish and Wildlife Service, Bureau of Commercial Fisheries.

Table A-6. *Puget Sound Salmon Landings, 1935–66*[a]

(*thousand pounds*)

Year	Chinook	Chum	Pink	Silver	Sockeye	Total
1935	4,827	7,186	33,490	12,209	4,262	61,974
1936	6,323	7,841	142	6,153	2,935	23,395
1937	5,587	7,743	29,241	6,626	6,183	55,380
1938	3,595	8,022	45	4,639	9,824	26,125
1939	3,907	3,309	23,372	7,046	3,838	41,472
1940	6,232	6,225	149	5,911	4,290	22,806
1941	5,127	6,732	11,619	6,932	10,091	40,501
1942	3,839	6,441	82	2,812	20,422	33,596
1943	4,228	3,962	5,594	4,675	1,660	20,120
1944	3,329	3,208	25	3,362	2,105	12,029
1945	4,175	4,206	33,880	5,263	4,627	52,152
1946	5,338	12,509	1	2,703	21,693	42,244
1947	4,939	5,773	53,951	7,441	570	72,675
1948	3,409	9,092	2	5,914	6,141	24,557
1949	4,113	4,303	44,210	6,886	6,165	65,677
1950	3,581	10,340	45	8,806	8,347	31,120
1951	3,113	9,428	33,943	6,776	7,821	61,081
1952	4,340	10,050	10	10,522	7,860	32,781
1953	4,424	4,072	34,225	6,325	12,370	61,416
1954	4,103	5,186	1	3,500	34,581	47,371
1955	3,327	2,614	31,386	5,315	6,071	48,713
1956	2,883	1,228	4	7,623	5,854	17,592
1957	4,143	1,184	17,264	4,180	8,663	35,435
1958	2,895	4,553	23	5,862	32,259	45,591
1959	2,960	4,342	13,566	4,075	9,643	34,586
1960	2,065	1,339	10	1,364	6,609	11,387
1961	2,640	1,523	4,809	5,136	8,104	22,213
1962	1,966	1,923	26	5,524	4,968	14,408
1963	2,734	2,831	30,318	3,076	7,578	46,537
1964	2,356	2,676	43	5,256	2,983	13,315
1965	1,941	1,798	4,563	3,466	5,917	17,685
1966	2,034	4,008	143	4,858	9,012	20,055

[a] Table includes fish landed from offshore waters.

Source: Annual Reports, State of Washington, 1960–67, Department of Fisheries (1960 issue contains historical summary).

Table A–7. Catch by Species, Puget Sound, 1913–66[a]

(*thousands of fish*)

Year	Chinook	Chum	Pink	Silver	Sockeye	Total
1913	290	605	15,908	1,225	21,599	39,627
1914	426	1,686	75	1,499	3,451	7,138
1915	301	1,884	7,369	1,109	804	11,467
1916	301	1,884	68	1,109	804	4,167
1917	441	1,095	13,345	936	4,962	20,779
1918	477	1,157	78	1,638	561	3,911
1919	348	1,475	4,668	1,363	747	8,601
1920	218	683	20	569	653	2,197
1921	269	270	4,402	762	1,135	6,838
1922	208	502	32	892	506	2,141
1923	225	638	5,534	887	482	7,766
1924	246	860	100	947	747	2,899
1925	284	535	6,665	869	1,243	9,596
1926	253	1,064	24	703	432	2,476
1927	288	527	6,526	1,029	988	9,357
1928	243	1,044	9	761	609	2,666
1929	312	1,486	7,433	807	1,248	11,286
1930	280	1,011	17	575	3,327	5,121
1931	208	682	8,132	513	723	10,258
1932	180	1,092	9	457	819	2,556
1933	211	504	6,040	536	1,575	8,866
1934	209	867	13	451	2,648	4,189
1935	76	719	4,994	577	535	6,901
1936	79	783	6	247	452	1,567
1937	93	774	4,168	348	870	6,253
1938	58	802	8	321	1,408	2,598
1939	61	331	3,946	359	548	5,244
1940	71	565	5	261	652	1,554
1941	72	673	1,452	276	1,548	4,020
1942	42	644	2	180	2,923	3,791
1943	57	396	757	218	196	1,624
1944	68	320	4	299	326	1,018
1945	88	421	5,769	389	718	7,375
1946	62	1,251	–	206	3,100	4,619
1947	37	595	9,274	469	76	10,451
1948	41	941	–	371	922	2,275
1949	52	440	6,755	426	909	8,581
1950	46	887	10	606	1,217	2,766
1951	52	796	5,393	423	1,129	7,793
1952	60	773	2	654	1,114	2,601

Table A–7 (continued)

Year	Chinook	Chum	Pink	Silver	Sockeye	Total
1953	59	346	5,360	342	1,961	8,067
1954	59	423	–	214	4,758	5,454
1955	57	212	3,838	300	934	5,313
1956	46	105	–	409	900	1,461
1957	49	103	2,986	294	1,689	5,121
1958	50	421	3	352	5,255	6,081
1959	55	361	2,427	348	1,808	4,999
1960	65	135	–	104	1,191	1,495
1961	81	133	688	384	1,378	2,664
1962	48	174	–	414	754	1,391
1963	94	295	5,672	233	1,315	7,609
1964	75	247	–	402	463	1,188
1965	96	192	624	405	1,023	2,340
1966	102	402	–	634	1,339	2,477

[a] Puget Sound includes U.S. waters inside and east of Neah Bay. Cape Flattery seine, gill net, and troll catches are excluded from this table.

Source: Annual Reports, State of Washington, 1960–67, Department of Fisheries (1960 issue contains historical summary).

Table A–8. Estimated Annual Sport Catches and Effort on Strait of Juan de Fuca, the San Juan Islands, and Inner Puget Sound, 1946–66[a]

		Number of salmon caught		
Year	Angler trips	Chinook	Coho	Total[b] salmon
1946	316,000	61,000	107,100	168,100
1947	343,000	82,400	120,100	221,700
1948	n.a.	n.a.	n.a.	n.a.
1949	531,300	92,500	214,800	395,400
1950	536,800	98,100	198,500	296,600
1951	609,500	131,700	208,900	369,200
1952	650,600	147,800	230,500	378,300
1953	631,700	121,400	190,200	385,500
1954	697,600	179,400	208,600	388,000
1955	695,800	163,400	214,400	467,900
1956	757,200	207,700	248,900	456,600
1957	775,900	251,000	301,500	631,500
1958	647,100	165,100	203,600	368,700
1959	577,200	122,600	160,500	322,300
1960	600,800	105,200	53,200	158,400
1961	775,900	132,000	122,300	291,800
1962	845,100	129,200	114,400	244,000
1963	1,157,100	175,300	178,000	773,800
1964	978,100	108,500	112,800	221,300
1965	961,912	117,599	149,471	306,957
1966	840,642	136,218	158,148	294,366

n.a. Not available.

[a] Washington Marine Waters adjacent to Cape Flattery and eastward, excluding the Pacific Ocean to the south.

[b] Includes pink and chum.

Source: Development of Washington State Salmon Sport Fishery Through 1964, State of Washington, Department of Fisheries. Fisheries Research Bulletin No. 7, May 1967. *Washington State Sport Catch Report from Punch Card Returns*, 1965, 1966, (mimeo.) State of Washington, Department of Fisheries, May, 1966–67.

Table A-9. Number of Licenses Issued for Salmon Fishing in Puget Sound, 1935–66

Year	Purse seine	Gill net	Reef net
1935	215	325	20
1936	172	323	49
1937	213	420	49
1938	230	453	74
1939	191	450	78
1940	158	381	76
1941	158	392	89
1942	154	263	70
1943	178	338	58
1944	88	284	46
1945	121	339	47
1946	167	325	64
1947	210	429	56
1948	255	485	92
1949	322	641	137
1950	317	472	126
1951	325	508	122
1952	278	445	101
1953	334	606	131
1954	310	631	102
1955	375	830	110
1956	211	706	86
1957	421	887	93
1958	447	953	107
1959	425	876	104
1960	338	812	89
1961	452	856	100
1962	386	827	75
1963	431	886	83
1964	293	787	63
1965	400	906	76
1966	317	835	52

Source: State of Washington, Department of Fisheries, Annual Reports.

Index

*References to figures and tables
are in italics.*

213